To Barb,
We treasure
friendship!
All our Best,

NO

CONDITION

IS PERMANENT

A Collection of Memories

Delano E. Lewis

with Brian Lewis

Delano E. Lewis

August, 2018

Copyright Notice

DEDICATION

This book is dedicated to my 11 grandchildren and 1 granddaughter-in-law:

Geoffrey Jr., Clinton, Justin, Abigail, Serina, Paulina, Tristan, Trey (Delano Lewis III), Piper, Claire, Annie and Dylan.

I hope you will find my memories helpful and educational as you move forward in your lives. I am proud to be a husband, father and grandfather to the amazing Lewis Family!

TABLE OF CONTENTS

Foreword by
Don Graham

Reader: I am pretty sure that if you read much of this book, you will find yourself saying: "This guy is too good to be true."

Yes.

That's what the friends of Del Lewis have spent their lives saying. A success in business, in politics, as a husband and as a father, Del is a little hard to believe.

Here's something still more unbelievable: Del's continual success and his reputation for brains, reliability and decency might easily have left a trail of jealous people and of rivals. That didn't happen.

For one thing, Del was never consumed by ambition. He took time to actually do the jobs he had—Peace Corps country manager, telephone company executive, president of National Public Radio—before going on to the next one.

I met Del when we were both young business executives—he with the Chesapeake and Potomac Telephone Company and I with The Washington Post—in a Washington just recovering from the 1968 riots.

There were people who were respected in DC's white community and others who were respected in its much larger African American community. A tiny number were respected in both, and Del Lewis would have led that list.

In a life filled with events, Del leaves out quite a few. He was a director of Apple Computer in the mid-1990's. That doesn't even make the book, and his other corporate directorships don't either.

In a very short chapter of this book, Del tells how an experienced politician suggested he might one day be the Vice-President of the United States—if he just ran for mayor of Washington first. I'm not sure that was at all unrealistic.

Many people in Washington wanted—maybe even prayed for—Del to run against Marion Barry (Mayor Barry is one of several people who is treated more kindly in Del's book than he deserved). In this book, Del confirms the story we all heard at the time—that his magnificent wife Gayle put her foot down and told him he wasn't going to be a political candidate.

It is interesting to ask oneself what might have happened if Gayle had leaned the other way. I think Del would have been quite likely to win a race for mayor. But it's not a job that has made any incumbent happy in my lifetime. Perhaps Gayle was wise.

Del, born in 1938, lived to see a very different America than the one he grew up in. He served on the staff of the first African American U.S. Senator since Reconstruction, Edward Brooke; became the first African American president of NPR; served as U.S. Ambassador to a post-Mandela South Africa; and raised wonderful children.

If you do not know Delano Lewis, I envy you the chance to learn about him in this book. He is a man worth knowing, and worth knowing about. Congratulations to Brian Lewis if he helped talk his Dad into setting down these memories.

PROLOGUE
FRAGILE - HANDLE WITH CARE

In August 1970 I resettled with my family in Washington DC. I first fell in love with this city in 1963 when I came after accepting a position in the Internal Security Division of the Department of Justice. I was a "brand new" lawyer and looking forward to using my law degree. We as a family were looking forward to living in Washington. I was excited about this move and anxious to begin a serious work career. For us as a family, this move was just one of many adventures we would share.

In 1966 I was offered the opportunity to work for the United States Peace Corps in Africa. I was reluctant to leave Washington and at the same time looking at the opportunities and adventures in store for us by accepting this challenge. We lived in Nigeria for one year and in Uganda for two years.

When we returned to Washington, I continued to work for the Peace Corps as Director of East and Southern Africa. It was a very good job, but not as exciting as in the field where I interacted with people. I needed to feel like I was making a difference.

It wasn't long before politics began calling my name. I was offered a job in the office of Senator Edward Brooke, the first African American elected to the United States Senate since Reconstruction. I was hired as a legislative assistant to develop legislation on social issues such as education, social security and welfare. This was an awesome opportunity and responsibility. His office was in the Old Senate Office Building, sometimes called the O.S.O.B. on Capitol Hill. Senator Brooke, a Republican, represented the State of Massachusetts. This was a very exciting time in my life.

My days began early and ended late. The radio alarm clock tuned to the morning news awoke me at 5:00 a.m. Each morning I would look into my closet and pick out the perfect suit to start my day. I would find a matching tie, and a perfectly starched shirt and coordinated belt to match. I, like my father, always wanted to be perfectly dressed. Finally, I would put on a pair of my favorite wingtip shoes that I had taken the time to polish the night before. I was 31-years old, tall and slender weighing about 170 pounds. I was young, energetic and had a positive vision of the future.

We only owned one car. Gayle needed the car to get the kids to and from school; therefore, I relied on public transportation. The car we owned was a 1968 Volkswagen bus. We bought it by mail from "Europe By Car" mail-order company. We chose our model and color from a catalogue. We paid for it by check and arranged to have it delivered to us in Lisbon, Portugal as we were traveling in Europe on our way home from the Peace Corps tour in Kampala, Uganda. The cost of the car was $1,500, basically our entire life savings. This was risky, but we took a leap of faith. Sure enough, our car was delivered to us in Lisbon, the exact model and tan color we picked out from the catalogue.

The easiest and least expensive mode of transportation for me was the city bus. The buses in Washington DC ran like clockwork. If I missed my regular bus in the morning, it could put me as much as twenty minutes behind schedule. On Capitol Hill, work was in full swing by 9 a.m. I preferred getting there early and I knew that I would only be comfortable if I arrived by 8:30 a.m. This meant I had to be out the door by 7:00

a.m. and no later. The first bus I normally caught would pick me up at my stop usually between 7:05 a.m. and 7:10 a.m. I had it down pat. I became acquainted with some of the bus drivers.

The 45-minute to an hour ride down to Capitol Hill was the perfect time for me to gather more of my thoughts. I would open my briefcase, pull out my yellow pad and pen and jot down notes to plan my day. I was always very organized and I had so many thoughts.

From time to time, I would gaze out the window and observe some of the culture of Washington. I loved it. Parts of the city still bore the scars of rioting that took place after the assassination of Martin Luther King in April of 1968. However, I saw a great city that could be rebuilt and prosper with the right leadership. I would dream and visualize myself as that leader. I knew early on that I had a gift to lead. I would always keep this dream close to my heart and in my thoughts.

On my way toward Capitol Hill, I would always glance over toward the White House and the Executive Office building. Secretly, I would be asking myself, what if I became the first black president? I had watched and followed and admired Martin Luther King Jr., a visionary leader. At the same time John and Robert Kennedy became role models for me on leadership and courage. Without a doubt, Senator Edward Brook was a living role model for me.

However, if I'm to be true, I often wondered if I had the disposition to deal with the criticism and controversy that came with moving the needle. I learned quickly that people in Washington who made things happen did not care if they were personally liked.

I had a hard time with that. I wanted to be liked and admired by everyone. I just kept telling myself that eventually everyone would come to like me; what was there not to like? The fact is, I was very fragile and if one thing scared me every day about politics in Washington, it was the fear of people talking about me behind my back.

In my short tenure as a practicing lawyer, I was a partner with an African American sole practitioner, P.A. Townsend of Topeka, Kansas. He was a general practitioner and a highly skilled and respected trial lawyer. While other legal opportunities were closed to me because of my race, I felt confident that I could learn from one of the best legal advocates in the country as was P.A. Townsend.

I did not aspire to be a criminal prosecutor but I did see myself as a criminal defense attorney. However, there were few opportunities in defense work where I could earn a living wage to support my family.

Senator Edward Brooke was a man with a quiet demeanor. He saw value in me and had great respect for my work career with the Peace Corps. I think he saw me as a rising star. I don't think he knew, nor did he care, that I was a Democrat. He had respect for all that I had achieved at such a young age. Having served at the Justice Department, and as a lawyer with The Equal Employment Opportunity Commission (EEOC) and having been in charge of Peace Corps programs in Nigeria and Uganda, gave me great experience in dealing with people. Add to this the fact that I was a trained lawyer with a social conscience and a desire to make a difference in society, Senator Brooke made the decision to hire me. He saw a young man who was hungry. Yes, I was hungry, and I had a mission.

I was first turned down for the legislative assistant position by the Administrative Assistant in the Senator's office, Alton Frye, who told me that the Senator's budget could not support the pay requirement that I needed. However, Senator Brooke himself intervened and called me in for an interview. After that interview, he offered me the job and at the salary I had requested.

As it happened, Senator Brooke and I were members of the same fraternity, Alpha Phi Alpha. In the summer of 1970, the fraternity held its annual meeting in Kansas City, my home area. Senator Brooke had been asked and agreed to be the keynote speaker at a major assembly. Knowing that I was from that area and knowing that we were fraternity brothers, he suggested I might join him in Kansas City for the occasion. I was honored and excited and realized that this would be a wonderful way to end the summer with family time.

We drove to Kansas City in our Volkswagen van, the one we had purchased through the mail and had delivered to us in Portugal. We were an attraction in our van. There were few, if any, such vehicles driving on the streets of Kansas City.

This was a very proud moment for my family and me as the Senator recognized me, a "hometown" fraternity brother and as a member of his staff.

In early October, my father called to let me know that my mother was in the hospital. She hadn't been feeling well when we were visiting but she chalked it up to a bad chest cold and maybe bronchitis. She had been coughing a lot so the doctors sent her to the hospital for tests. I asked my father to keep me posted on mom's illness. I figured that she would be fine and that dad had it all under control.

Something continued to gnaw at me. I wasn't sure what it was. I just couldn't pinpoint it, but something wasn't right. I had heard nothing back from my father, so I gave him a call. He told me that mom was still in the hospital and they were doing more tests. It was obvious at this time that the over-the-counter cold medicines, and whatever else she may have been taking, were not doing the trick.

I was now convinced that this was what had been gnawing at me. I was in fear that mom's sickness may be more serious than I had thought. I tried not to let this keep me from focusing on my new job, but this was my mother. She was my rock. She raised me. And when I say 'raised me,' she really raised me.

I hung up the phone and decided I would just wait to hear more news. There was not a whole lot I could do and I knew worrying would not change anything. Again, I had to trust that my dad had it all under control and would make good on his promise to keep me abreast of what was going on.

October of 1970, like most Octobers in Washington, was a beautiful month. The leaves were changing on the trees and it was a beautiful time to be in Washington. The temperature had finally dropped and the weather was now hovering around 65-70 degrees. My four sons were growing like weeds. We had them all enrolled in various schools to suit their personalities. My family was hitting its stride. I was very proud of myself being able to provide for my family and to give Gayle everything she had always wanted, which was to be a mother and to raise kids.

One evening as we were having dinner, my father called. This in itself was of concern because he seldom called. He told me that mom had been diagnosed with lung cancer and it appeared to be terminal. He told me that the doctors would do some treatment, but he was sure it probably would not do a whole lot of good. This was devastating. It rocked my world like no other thing. I wasn't sure what to do.

I talked to Gayle and she tried to calm me down and keep me at peace as I was having a rough time. It hit me hard, much harder than I had ever imagined. I had been trying to deny what I had felt when I last saw my mom in August. Maybe I was suppressing what I knew to be true, that she was very sick. My father's news was devastating. I just couldn't think straight.

I arranged with Senator Brooke to take some time off from work to go to Kansas City to be with my mom. I went directly to the hospital to spend time with her. I stayed a few days and we talked, but I could tell at this point she was very sick. Her coughing was still bad and it was so hard for me to listen to and so hard for me to watch her in pain.

At one point, I left her hospital room for a little while to track down doctors and ask them questions. I was so concerned about the coughing and was told by one doctor that they would try to give her some medication to ease the coughing, but the cancer was terminal and that they did not know how long she would live.

By now I was just trying to make sure she was comfortable. I could tell the coughing was hurting her and her pain was hurting me. Later that day, I left the hospital and spent time with my dad. He asked me what my plans were and I told him I wasn't sure how long I would stay. I think I caught my dad off guard because I believe he thought and expected me to help him with mom. But I knew I had my own family to tend to. I had a new job and I needed to be the provider. This meant getting back to work.

The next morning, I got up and told dad I just couldn't take it, that watching mom suffer was too much for me and that I would go back to DC. I told him it would be best if he would keep me posted on what was going on.

This was a very difficult decision for me. I wasn't sure if it was the right decision, but it's what I did. Once again, this was a symptom of my own fragility. I just couldn't stand to watch the woman who raised me suffer and to take her last breath. It was just best for me to move on. I went back to DC and I tried to drown myself in work and distract myself from the inevitable, one day at a time.

On Sunday, November 1, 1970, I got a call from my Aunt Julia, mom's older sister who also lived in Kansas City. She told me that my mom had passed away. This was devastating, yet, I remember thinking she was in a better place and that her passing would allow me to move on with my life.

I asked Aunt Julia how my dad was doing and she said he was holding up well. The inevitability of her dying finally happened and most of the family and friends in Kansas City were somewhat relieved that she was no longer suffering.

After hanging up the phone with my Aunt Julia, I sat down and cried like a baby. I've always been a crier and never ashamed to show my emotions. My mother was the only example of family I ever knew. Yes, my dad was in the picture, but in a very limited way. The comfort, love and security had come from my mother.

Later, the range of emotions that came over me was too much for me to bear. I had so many questions with so few answers. Why did my mother get sick? Is there no God? Did I do something wrong? Lung cancer? She never smoked a day in her life!

These thoughts were racing through my head. The one thing that stood out immediately was that my dad smoked. He smoked everything from pipes to cigars to non-filter Lucky Strike cigarettes. I'm thinking, was it his fault? Was the secondhand smoke to blame for her lung cancer? There was so much to process and it was all wrapped up in my fear and anger.

And then my own guilt took over my mind and I just couldn't shake it. My mother did everything for me. I would not be the man I am today if it were not for my mother. So the guilt I was feeling was connected to a sense of abandonment. I was thinking maybe I should have taken care of her or maybe I should have lived closer to watch over her.

After some time alone, Gayle comforted me and we talked. Together, we would get through this and we needed to plan for my next steps. My boss, Senator Brooke, already knew of my mother's illness so taking time away from the office to attend her funeral and burial was not an issue, nor a surprise, to him.

The funeral was set for Thursday, November 5th, and the burial was on Saturday, November 7th. Gayle and I talked about the whole family attending the service, but that made little sense. Our kids were still very young, ranging in ages from nine down to two, and they didn't know my mother that well. Our oldest son, Del Jr., may have remembered her the best.

The other reason for not packing up the family was because of finances. We were not rich by any means and we basically lived from paycheck to paycheck. We had just come from a family summer trip through Kansas City so money was tight. Therefore, I went back to Kansas to lay my mother to rest. She had been my rock and a central part of my life. I realized that she would no longer be suffering.

I arrived in Kansas City on Wednesday, November 4th. My dad and Aunt Julia picked me up and we went back to my childhood home at 1006 Freeman Avenue. I was still struggling with so much grief and there was a part of me that didn't want to face my fears. I had many fears about being an only child and having to answer many questions about mom. I had no brothers or sisters to divert the unwanted attention. What my mother and I had was special and I wanted it to stay that way.

When I entered the house, it smelled and looked very much like it did when I grew up there. It had a very homey and comfortable feeling with an underlying scent of pipe tobacco and I instantly felt mom's presence. She was everywhere in the house.

I zoned in on one particular photo of her that was on the table. In the picture, I could see her big, beautiful smile and her signature gap between her two front teeth. She had a lovely smile, pretty teeth, big, full lips and soft dimples above her cheekbones. My mother came from a very large family with nine sisters and two brothers. She and my father married shortly after she graduated from Arkansas City High School. She always wanted to be a nurse but her desire was stymied by her sisters who told her that she would never accomplish that goal because she was too dark.

As the day went on, some of the uneasiness and tension subsided. Dad and I talked at length about his plans going forward and about how he was feeling. My dad was not much on information, much less talking in general. He was a quiet man and I did not know him well. He was always well dressed, usually in a suit and tie, whatever the occasion. He always wore shoes that matched the color of his suit. He left Arkansas City High School after completing the 11th grade. He began working immediately thereafter. He had a very strong work ethic and never denied my mother or me anything. He always paid the bills and made sure there was a roof over our heads and food in the refrigerator. His very soft and quiet voice was as gentle as a beautiful whisper. He spoke with conviction when asked about his beliefs, about church, his work and his dress. He never shied away from a good game of dominoes and he always was the perfect gentleman.

After a restless and uncomfortable nights' sleep, the next morning arrived and we got ready and met with some of the other relatives. The funeral was held at the Eighth Street Baptist Church, which was the same church I attended as a child. The service was at 2 p.m. that afternoon.

The Eighth Street Baptist Church brought back many memories for me. I had left the congregation many years ago and had converted to Catholicism. The church appeared smaller than what I remember growing up. Although the gathering was fairly small, the presiding pastor led a good service.

On the day after, we gathered with other members of our family for a time of sharing stories and having dinner together. I remember there being a large spread of food and lots of chatter. My Kansas family had so many questions, asking me about Gayle and the kids and how I liked Washington DC. It was a welcome diversion.

On Saturday morning we packed our things and made the three-hour drive down to Arkansas City where mom was to be buried. This was a long ride and I was not looking forward to it. However, it gave me more time to make sure my dad had a plan. I asked him about some of mom's things and what he had planned to do with the house. As usual, I got very limited answers. I left that conversation alone and just tried to get through the weekend.

Once we arrived in "Ark City," the experience of being there was more emotional than I had expected. These emotions were not so much about my mom being gone, but more about flashbacks I was having of my early childhood times when visiting there. When I was a young boy in my teens, I remember my mom telling me a story about how and why we left Arkansas City.

She told me that when I was just two or three years old, we were living in Ark City and my dad had just found this great job in Kansas City. This was great for our family, but something told mom that when dad left for his new job three hours away, he might not be coming back.

But mom was having none of that. She was set on making this family union work and separation was not an option. Instead of waiting to see if dad would come back to us, she packed us up and followed dad to Kansas City.

This was a bold move on my mother's part, but one which I am very thankful for. My father was not the ideal father in a lot of ways, but having a dad who was a provider, working on the Santa Fe Railroad as a porter for thirty-seven years, helped shape me as a man in the long term.

Arkansas City was where my parents grew up and met. Their families were both from there.

Many years before I was born, there was a family burial lot purchased for mom. This was why we were here to bury her.

At the burial site, I began to reflect on my childhood and my many conversations with my mother as I was growing up. She was always there helping, guiding and directing me toward self-fulfillment. I would miss her affirmations.

For a moment, I felt frozen and alone. I was not sure if I was living up to my mother's grand expectations of me. Was I in the right career? What about my dad? Should I try to get closer to him now that she was gone?

As an only child and with a father who was away with his work, I was now faced with life on my own. With these insecurities and fears I knew I had to face these challenges squarely in order to survive.

On the way back home to DC, I did a lot more thinking. There were so many questions that had unfolded over the last four days; who I wanted to become and who I refused to become.

My abilities to communicate and understand others were two of the greatest gifts my mother gave me. But when I began to self-examine and seek my truth, I came to realize I was a fragile man now on his own.

My mother always understood her little boy. Her constant encouragement and overbearing nature was her way of masking the pain of so many shortcomings in our small, dysfunctional family. She knew I was fragile and she did her best to hold me together. Now that she was gone, I began to understand that her love provided the foundation for my own self-realization. Love for oneself is so critical to loving others. This is still a work in progress.

KEEPING UP
WITH THE JONESES

It's 5:00 a.m. and my alarm goes off. As I roll over to shut it off, I see the bright sun peeking through the bottom of my shaded window and I can hear the others moving around and about the Alpha Phi Alpha Fraternity House where I lived. I had just arrived back to campus after spending the summer working on the Great Northern Railroad and had saved enough money to buy my first car. It was a 1955 Chevy, turquoise and white, and I was the talk of the house.

I needed to get up and start my day waiting tables at the Gamma Phi Beta Sorority House. I was to be there by 6:00 a.m. We served breakfast at 6:30 a.m. and I was always on time and ready to go. This was a great job but proved to make for a long and exhausting day. Between waiting tables, classes and studying at the library, I didn't have much time for socializing.

In 1958 I was beginning my junior year at the University of Kansas (KU), in Lawrence, Kansas. There was a lot going on in 1958. The United States was in a recession and five million people were unemployed. The Federal minimum wage was $1 an hour and I remember a postage stamp was only four cents. A gallon of gas was roughly twenty-five cents. Our country was also involved in a war in Vietnam. I was fortunate at 19 to be in college with the support of my family. I had a job which I needed, but I didn't feel the same economic pinch that so many other students did.

My days were long and tiring beginning with work, attending classes, and work again in the evenings after classes. I stuck with my schedule of work, class, library study and always my routine nap. I scheduled a nap between 3:00 p.m. and 5:00 p.m. every day. I took my naptime seriously. I had been taking naps ever since I was a young boy and had mastered the art of the nap.

It wasn't long before the voices of the fraternity house were in full volume. This was my cue to get up and get ready to leave for work and study at Watson library. The house was filled with characters and practical jokesters, but we were all very studious.

Upon leaving the house one evening, I heard from my roommate, Reginald Buckner about a big sorority party coming up. Reg and I had been close for years and we always confided in one another. He asked me if I was going and if I had a date. I told him, no, I didn't have a date and asked him if he had one. He, too, was solo and we weren't sure if we wanted to show up stag.

Then Reg suggested I ask a student named Gayle Jones to the dance. I looked at him like he was crazy. I said, "Gayle Jones? Reg, she's way out of my league and she is much too smart."

"That might be true, Delano," he said with a smile on his face, "but there's only one way to find out."

I didn't give it much more thought and left the house headed for work and study. I couldn't focus on the books; I was busy thinking about all the ways to ask Gayle to the dance. I was even thinking about my Plan B if she said no.

Gayle and I met shortly after we both arrived on campus in the fall of 1956. She was a junior that year and I was a freshman. I knew of her, but mostly just about how smart she was. That was the most intimidating part. But I got the nerve up, picked up the house phone and made the call. I introduced myself, again, and politely asked her if she had a date for the dance. She told me no and then I asked her if she would like to go with me. Thankfully, she responded yes, and I was in heaven. This was fantastic.

About an hour later, the unthinkable happened. The house phone rang and the ring tone was clear – it was two longs and a short. I picked up the phone and it was Gayle. My stomach dropped, as I knew I was about to get dumped even before our first date. She said, "Delano, did you just call me a while ago and ask me to the dance?"

I said, "Yes, Gayle, I did, and let me remind you that you said yes."

She quickly said, "Oh no, I'm very committed to going with you. I was taking a nap when you called before and I wanted to make sure I was not imagining our conversation." I was quite relieved.

Throughout the week leading up to the dance, Gayle and I continued to communicate. Our conversations seemed to get longer and more interesting. I was learning so much about her and her family and I was feeling comfortable about our first date. Since it was a dance, I thought it important to ask her whether she just wanted to be social or if she enjoyed dancing. She said that she loved music and enjoyed the atmosphere, but wasn't real big on dancing.

Well, this was both good news and bad news for me. The good news was that I finally felt I could do something better than Gayle which helped my self-esteem, but the bad news was I might not have anyone to dance with while there.

Word got out around the fraternity I was going to the dance with Gayle Jones. Many of my frat brothers were happy for me and some were jealous. Reginald, however, was like a proud father who had made a match come to reality.

My first date with Gayle was wonderful. We had a great time and with Gayle's permission, I danced with others. She was comfortable in her own skin and when I returned after each dance, she was there waiting. She was also a good dancer.

This was a good sign. I knew that night Gayle Jones was special. She was very pleasant and easy to talk to. This was very important. I knew I needed someone who was a good listener and someone who could challenge me. Gayle saw me for me and enjoyed who I was.

Our conversations over the next year grew deeper. I talked a lot about my family and I learned a lot about hers. She was raised as a Catholic and had three siblings. I was raised Baptist and had no siblings. The more I got to know Gayle, the more I realized how different we were. She had this strong family unit and had traveled in the States with her family on vacations. She was very smart, entering college at the bright young age of fourteen. Sometimes, because our worlds were so different, I wasn't sure if this would work, but our dating continued and the relationship deepened.

We studied together and became a real strong couple. I knew this was love and that while I may not be as smart as Gayle, I was smart enough to not let her get away. With having a new love in my life, working and studying, the time just flew by. Christmas of 1958 was fast approaching and I knew this would be our first Christmas shared as a couple.

I discovered that I could work over the holiday on the Great Northern Railroad as a waiter to make extra cash. This was great news and right on time. I had been thinking about my steps with Gayle and wanted to make sure I kept dating and kept my car filled with gas. The whole time I was away over Christmas, I wrote Gayle and told her how much I missed her. We had talked some about marriage but nothing definitive yet. It was on my radar but I wanted to have a secure plan for my future before I took that step.

Gayle and I made it through the holiday season of 1958 and were looking forward to the upcoming year. The economy was picking up and I was looking forward to finishing my junior year at KU.

In the year 1959, things started to escalate between Gayle and me. We were now talking about marriage and a wonderful life together. But first things first, I needed to finish school.

I told Gayle I had plans to attend law school after KU. She was very supportive of this while positively thinking about grad school for herself. This seemed like the perfect plan until one particular night when we were studying in our favorite spot in Strong Hall. I remember telling Gayle how excited I was about our future together and contemplating what law school to attend. I was considering the law school at KU or the Washburn School of Law in Topeka.

After I finished telling Gayle of my quandary, I looked at her and I said, "Honey, what do you want to do with your life?"

She kind of looked at me with a straight face and made a no-nonsense reply. Gayle said, "I want to get married and have babies."

Uh oh, I'm thinking to myself, this was not in my plan. How could I go to law school and raise a family simultaneously? I looked at Gayle with reassurance that somehow, if that's what she wanted, we would make it work. Meanwhile, deep inside I was scared, very scared.

After that conversation, I knew I would do anything to be with Gayle. She was my best friend and I loved her dearly. I spent the summer of 1959 working on the Great Northern railroad saving my money for marriage. I missed Gayle so much!

Since I had earned enough credits to graduate in my senior year, June 1960, I took a course at the KU Law School. Soon thereafter, I made the choice to attend Washburn Law School in Topeka.

BREAKING THE NEWS

In early May of 1959, Gayle conversed with her father by phone in Texas. She explained to her dad she was in love with this wonderful, good-looking, smart and aspiring lawyer (slight embellishment), and that they were thinking about one day getting married.

Her father, Herman T. Jones, a very practical and thoughtful man, told Gayle, "Not so fast." Gayle was taken aback by this, but then her father explained.

He said, "Listen, you have been in college since you were fourteen years old. I see that you are having a good time and are taking a class or two here and there, but that's just not acceptable. I will not give my blessing on any marriage until after you have gained your degree."

This was no surprise to Gayle. Both of her parents were educators and her sister was studying to become a teacher. Getting her degree was a must. Mr. Jones then said he had a good plan for Gayle. He suggested she come home to Prairie View, Texas, to finish her degree at Prairie View

A&M. Her father was a professor at the university and this seemed to make sense, both educationally and economically.

Later in the week, after much anticipation on Gayle's part, she told me what her father had suggested. Neither of us wanted to be apart from each other for the academic year, '59-'60, but we both agreed it would be best.

I told Gayle I would find time to get to Texas over the year to visit. I also agreed to the plan because I knew that one day I would need the blessing of her father and I didn't want to screw this up. So I encouraged Gayle to do as her father suggested. She quickly looked at the course schedule at Prairie View and planned the quickest route to a degree. She settled on economics which was the fastest avenue to complete her college degree.

The summer of 1959 arrived and we were apart for the first time since we met. It felt odd and lonely. I was worried that Gayle may not miss me as much as I missed her, but the daily letters I received from her soon eased that. We were making this long distance relationship work and our plan for the future was intact and taking beautiful shape.

On November 12, 1959, I turned twenty-one. In today's world this would be a real big deal, having the right to drink and go to clubs. It would be considered something special. However, this did not interest me. I was much more focused on graduation and then getting admitted to law school.

I remember getting a nice letter from Gayle wishing me a happy birthday and encouraging me to have fun. Birthdays in general have always been special to me, especially my own. There's just something about celebrating another year of my life and looking forward, rather than looking backward. Perhaps it all started from my mother when I was a child. She would make a big deal about my birthdays and spoil me rotten. Whatever the case, I just love the day of my birth.

However, this one was extra special. I was counting down the days until I would see Gayle. We had arranged for her to meet me in Kansas City at my parents' home for Thanksgiving. We would stay with my mom and dad and I couldn't wait.

Both my mother and father knew all about Gayle and were very accepting of this new love in my life. My mom was maybe a little bit overprotective and felt as if she was losing her little boy. My father was as cool as can be and just took it all in. I will never forget the conversation we had about my wanting to get married.

On that day, I was sitting with my dad. He was in his lounge chair, in his dress clothes and polished shoes looking sharp as a tack. Now, nothing is wrong with wearing dress clothes and nice shoes, except we were at home and it was 7 or 8 p.m. in the evening. One would think he would put on something more relaxing, but after many years I had learned this *was* relaxing for my dad. I remember that he had his favorite pipe in his mouth, the end of it worn from his teeth. There was something intimidating about this beautiful brown polished pipe sticking out beyond his big, ruby red lips. I said, "Dad?"

He said, "Yah, D?" (My dad called me 'D' every so often.)

I said, "I think I want to get married."

He looked up at me as his eyes grew closer together looking puzzled and confused, inhaled, and out of the side of his mouth came a puff of smoke. Then he said, "D, married? Why do you want to do that?" This was typical dad.

I replied, "I'm in love." I wasn't sure what his reaction would be, but the one I got was not surprising.

The conversation continued and I told him I had been accepted to law school at Washburn in Topeka. I was curious for his reaction, reason being my father had said many months ago when I first mentioned law school to him that he would help pay for it. But now that I had dropped the marriage bomb on him, I didn't know what to expect.

Two minutes went by and another puff of smoke filled the air. This time he pulled the pipe from his mouth and said, "D, I told you that I would help you with law school and I still will."

I said, "Dad, really?"

He said, "Son, I gave you my word and I will honor it to help." I was jumping for joy. I couldn't believe it. This meant so much because deep down I knew that Gayle just wanted to get married and have babies and that was *not* information I would share with dad that night.

Thanksgiving could not arrive fast enough. I had a plan and I couldn't wait to execute it. Before leaving campus for Thanksgiving, I spoke to my two roommates, Kenton Keith and Reginald Buckner, about my plan. I told them that Gayle and I had been talking marriage for some time, but over the holiday I would make it official. They both were very happy and supportive.

I had picked out a ring helped by my mother several months prior. Upon saving my money and planning this perfectly, I purchased the ring and ask Gayle to marry me. Both my mother and father knew about the plan and were excited to have it happen at their home. Although this was a very big deal for me and for Gayle, it was almost a foregone conclusion. We had talked about this so much in our letters to each other that this proposal would not be a huge shock to Gayle. In one of the latest letters I had sent her, I spoke about starting a family and even talked about names for our children. I knew I wanted to have a Delano, Jr., and I even told Gayle I loved the name Gayle Carolyn, and we could name one daughter after her. I was prepared and it was no mystery about what Gayle's answer would be.

It was a short visit over Thanksgiving and everything turned out great, except the engagement ring was too big. Other than that, she said yes and the planning began. I was a little bit worried about my mother and her need to know everything about Gayle and her family. This would be a big deal.

Gayle's family was different, very liberal and very worldly. While in Kansas City, Gayle suggested I make a trip to Texas for the Christmas break. She said it would be a good idea if I spent time with her family and celebrated the good news and I agreed. It was only three weeks away and I was excited.

In December 1959 I took the train to Texas. It was the cheapest way to get there because of my father's job with the Santa Fe Railroad. My mother and I had Rail Passes to travel free on Santa Fe trains. I loved riding the train and especially this time since it was to see Gayle and spend time with her family over Christmas.

I arrived by train on an unusually chilly Texas afternoon at Bellville Railroad Yard, a tiny

Santa Fe railway station about 20 miles southwest of Prairie View. When we arrived at her home, I met Gayle's mother, her grandmother who lived with the family, her brother Ralph who was there from California for the holidays, and her younger sister Pat. Her sister Jan, whom I knew from KU days, was home from Mexico City College where she was studying for a Master's degree.

Gayle's parents' house was located on the campus of Prairie View A&M. It was a nice, medium-sized and comfortable home with a large yard with lots of room to relax or just play catch with a Frisbee. I was excited to be there.

The Jones Family was very excited to see me and they even planned an engagement party for the two of us. This was special. I had heard so much about her parents, but never had long talks with them before. I knew I would have to put my best foot forward.

Gayle's father, Herman T. Jones, was a fairly dark-skinned man who stood at about 5'10" and wore a goatee. I remember on that day he was casually dressed and stood sure of himself. The tone of his voice was pleasurable and he spoke with a quiet confidence. Each word of his vocabulary seemed to flow beautifully. He loved words, languages and learning something new each day. He was well traveled and would literally give you the shirt off his back if you were in need.

Gayle's mom, Gwendolyn Jones, stood about 5'4" and had a medium build. She, like Gayle's father, was an educator. She taught special needs children and loved it. She was a very wise woman who could see the truth right through you. For me, the most interesting fact about Gayle's mom was her family history. Mrs. Jones was a woman who came from Canadian, Irish and African roots. This meant Gayle was the child of a mixed ancestry. Before I continue, let me remind you that this is 1959 and Gayle's mom and dad got married in 1935. No wonder they weren't afraid of anything or anyone!

As the party was going on in full bloom and everyone was congratulating us, the unthinkable happened! After pulling me aside, Gayle's mom says, "Do you realize that this engagement is not official?"

I looked at her with obvious panic and said, "Mrs. Jones, what do you mean?"

She said, "You have to ask Gayle's father for her hand in marriage."

I looked softly down at her light brown eyes and said, "Oh my, I thought that tradition had been long gone." She told me no and if I wanted this engagement to be official, she suggested I find Mr. Jones and ask him right now for Gayle's hand in marriage.

So off I went in search of Gayle's father. I knew the deal he had made with Gayle about not blessing the marriage until after she had graduated and that had not happened yet, so part of me was a little concerned on what his response would be. I finally found Mr. Jones and gently approached him.

I began the conversation with, "I am very much in love with your daughter and I will take very good care of her." I continued on as if I was applying for a job. I told him what my plans were for the future, how I intended to go to law school, where Gayle and I would reside after marriage, and how I intended to be the primary income source, and so forth and so on.

He looked at me with his very intellectual face and dark, high cheekbones. I looked up, not into his glaring, intimidating brown eyes, but focused in on the shiny bald patch on the top of his head.

He said, "Well, Delano, you know we are Catholic. What are you two doing about faith? Faith is very important."

I told him I was converting to Catholicism and had taken classes. He was pleased. Finally, and to my relief, he said, "Okay, Delano, I honor your request to take my daughter's hand in marriage."

We had a wonderful hug and that's when I knew the Jones Family accepted me.

PEACE CORPS
TAKING MY LEAP OF FAITH

> **"Faith is taking the first step, even when you can't see the whole staircase."**
>
> *- Dr. Martin Luther King, Jr.*

"This is Pan American Flight 150, final destination, Lagos, Nigeria. Flight time will be approximately 12 hours."

I was sitting on the plane next to my wife, Gayle, and my youngest son, Brian. My two other sons, Geoffrey and Del Jr., were in seats across the aisle from me. Even traveling economy as all government employees did, I can remember the aisles were wide enough for passengers to stand and walk around in order to stretch.

For the kids and Gayle this was a real adventure, a road trip beyond road trips. But for me, it was a little unsettling. I was testing my faith and my fear was setting in. I was about to embark on the most unpredictable move of my life. To be honest, I was fearful of the unknown, but that was nothing compared to the fear I had of the known. And what I knew was enough to make any young family man question his sanity for a moment or two.

I was on my way to Benin City, Nigeria, where I was to be in charge of hundreds of Peace Corps volunteers, none of whom I knew. It would be my responsibility to lead all those volunteers and help them navigate their way through their assignments in West Africa.

As I periodically gazed out the window of the airplane into the pitch-black darkness, I kept pondering all the questions racing through my mind. Who was *I* to think anybody would listen to a rookie Peace Corps staffer? Why would they follow *my* lead? Did *I* have what it would take?

Even though this was a family venture, sometimes I felt alone and maybe crazy. I was a 27-year-old man, a lawyer, and I was gaining momentum and career status. Then one day out of the blue I was presented with an amazing opportunity. I was offered the position of Associate Director of the Peace Corps program in the Midwest region of Nigeria.

So there I was, hovering over the Atlantic Ocean at 30,000 feet with my wife, three children all under the age of six, traveling 6,500 miles from our home. How in the world did this come about?

This adventure started in Washington DC in 1963. We lived in a small apartment on Ames Street in the northeast part of the city. There was nothing special about our living quarters except that we were comfortable and had a roof over our heads. It was just enough for Gayle, my three sons, Del Jr., Geoff, Brian, and me.

On one particular morning in the fall, I got ready for work as usual. After I greeted Gayle with a good morning kiss on her cheek, I reminded her that I wouldn't need my bag lunch. "Today is my meeting with Roger Bernique and we're having lunch at his house."

"Oh, that's right," Gayle says. "Today is your big luncheon with the senior attorney". I shook my head yes, checked myself one last time in the small mirror near the front door, kissed my three little sons goodbye, and off to work I went.

This was a big day for me. I was new at the Department of Justice working as an attorney in the Internal Security Division. Mr. Bernique, a Senior Attorney, was always interested in the up and coming new lawyers in the department. He often invited new attorneys to his home for lunch. He wanted to get to know us as people as well as new lawyers. Some of the other new lawyers had been invited to Mr. Bernique's home for lunch, but now it was my turn. I was excited about going to lunch at Roger's home to get to know him better and to get to meet his wife as well.

Roger Bernique was a French/Canadian American man, probably in his early 40's. He was a kind, soft-spoken and very inquisitive. He was intrigued by the thoughts of others, their desires and their dreams, and I was more than willing to share mine.

It was a little before lunchtime when Roger and I arrived at his home. I met his wife, Terese, who was there waiting to greet us. She was a lovely woman, fairly small in build and in her late 30's. She, too, was of French/Canadian American decent. Roger and Terese were a delightful couple. I can still recall entering the front door and the aroma of a delicious meal. I remember thinking to myself, this is great, a day off from peanut butter and jelly.

Roger invited me to sit down in the living area and offered me a drink. At first, our conversation was only small talk and nervous jibber jabber, but I slowly began to get more relaxed and comfortable. I asked him about his home and how long he had lived there. I don't remember his response, but I remember the house. It was on Massachusetts Avenue in a wonderful area of DC. It was very nice and not far from embassy row where many of the foreign embassies in Washington are located.

We got comfortable with one another and I opened up. I couldn't help but think that someday Gayle and I could live in a house like this. I enjoyed his home and the neighborhood. Lunch was going great and Terese joined us. We laughed and talked about everything from jobs, my time in Kansas and my family.

When we were finished eating, both Roger and Terese commented on how much I had talked about my family, especially Gayle. I told them she was the love of my life and they said that they would very much like to meet her.

Later that year, I moved on and got a new job with the Equal Employment Opportunity Commission, called the EEOC. I kept in contact with Roger, letting him know what I was up to and how my family was doing.

In January of 1966, we moved from our small apartment on Ames Street into a townhouse in Seat Pleasant, Maryland, just outside of Washington DC. Not only was the housing more affordable, the extra square footage gave us some much-needed room. Back in July of '64, we had become a family of five when our third son, Brian, was born.

Then one day, Gayle received an unexpected phone call from Terese Bernique. She was calling to invite Gayle and me over for a dinner party the following week. When I arrived home that evening, Gayle shared the good news and we were both very excited. Our house was still a mess with boxes everywhere from moving so we needed to get out of the house. Gayle immediately went on a mission to find a babysitter for the sons. She told me she had met the next-door neighbors when we first moved in and they had teenage daughters always looking to make a buck or two, so we hired them to watch our sons.

The dinner party was to begin around 6:00 p.m. and it was about a thirty-minute drive to the

Bernique home. It was January and it was cold. Around 4:45 p.m., I knew we needed to get a move on. I ran out to our 1958 Plymouth that we had acquired from Gayle's parents and started the car to get the heat going while Gayle was instructing the babysitters and off we went.

During our drive, I was telling Gayle all about the Bernique's house and how I loved the neighborhood. She was excited for a night out and away from the daily grind of motherhood. The drive took us over thirty minutes and we arrived at 5:45 p.m. Perfect, I'm thinking, right on time. We rang the doorbell and were met by Roger and Terese. They were happy to see us and delighted we made it.

Three other couples had been invited to dinner as well. After introductions, we chatted over hors d'oeuvres and enjoyed drinks. During dinner, the conversation turned to business, law and Washington politics, led by Roger himself. I felt that Roger was very supportive of me and the other new lawyers at Justice and he wanted us to continue to strive forward and to make a difference in society.

As the conversation circled the dinner table with each individual taking a moment to give his or her thoughts about whatever the topic was, something out of the blue happened. When the conversation moved to government agencies, the woman sitting beside me, turned to me and asked, "Delano, how would you like to go to Africa?"

The woman's name was Cynthia Courtney and she was a close friend of the Bernique's. At first I wasn't sure if I heard the question correctly, but before I could say *pardon*, she repeated herself. She said, "How would you like to go to Africa?" Okay, this time I heard her and lucky for me, I had no sip of wine in my mouth or I might have choked. Gayle was all ears and wanted to hear more.

I took one look at Cynthia and said, "Did you say Africa? I am fresh out of Kansas. How could I go to Africa?" By this point, both Gayle and I are looking at her like this must be a joke just waiting for the punch line to come.

Cynthia looked at Gayle and me and said, "You could go with the United States Peace Corps." I just smiled and shook my head in bewilderment. Part of me wanted to say, "Don't you know I have a law degree?"

But I kept my cool and politely said, "Well, it has always been my understanding that the Peace Corps was a volunteer organization made up mostly of college graduates with bachelor degrees. I have a family I must support so I couldn't do that."

Cynthia, calmly, put all of my concerns to rest and said that if I was interested I could go as part of the Peace Corps staff. She said that being employed as Peace Corps staff would be a paid position and that I would be an employee of the Federal government. I could also bring my family and would be provided with housing. At that moment I was speechless while Gayle was thinking about the possibilities.

It's now getting late and we needed get home, relieve the babysitters, and get to bed ourselves. Before leaving the party on our way out, Cynthia came up to me and said, "Delano, I think this is a really good opportunity that you should think seriously about. Here is my card. Please call me if you have any more questions and I will be glad to set up a meeting with you at my office." I thanked her and then looked down at her card. It read, *Cynthia Courtney, Desk Officer, West Africa, United States Peace Corps, Washington DC*.

The ride home from the party was filled with conversation about what had just taken place. Gayle's thoughts and ideas of what had just happened were amazing. I could hear something in her voice as we were driving home. She had this "why not?" and "live and let live" tone as she was speaking. She was delicately encouraging me to think more outside the box.

This whole offer came out of nowhere. I had just recently graduated from law school and had spent three years learning how to think differently. My whole brain was now trained to do my due diligence and then do it again. Gayle was in the "let's go for it, you only live once!" frame of mind. This would be tough.

Upon sleeping on this offer and trying to put it on the back burner, it just wouldn't go away. I was excited and I knew Gayle was all for it, but I just wasn't sure if it made good sense to me. Here I was in a great city, the Nation's Capital, making my mark as a young attorney. I was making a living and we were surviving. It was 1966 and I just couldn't ask for more. I had thoughts about one day returning to the Midwest and now all of a sudden my life flipped upside down.

After about a week, I got up one morning and told Gayle I would call Cynthia. My thought process at this point was that it couldn't hurt to get all the details. Frankly, I was sure that I would run into some deal breaker and that Gayle and I would agree to just stay put.

Later that day, I made the call and set up a meeting. I was curious, excited and knew that I was in the driver's seat. When I got to the meeting Cynthia was pleased to see me. We went into her office and she explained all about the position. I knew that I would not make a final decision that day and not without briefing Gayle first.

Cynthia explained that I would be a leader. *She had my attention.* She told me that with this experience on my resume, I could write my own ticket in Washington. *Now she had even more of my attention.* Then she said that if I was ready, there was a possible opening in the next six months to be stationed in BO Sierra Leone. "Wow," I said, "this is moving pretty quickly."

She replied, "Yes, if you are ready, then we want you." All I can say is there is something special about knowing you are wanted. It makes you stop and think.

When I got home from work that night, Gayle was feeding the kids and doing laundry while simultaneously unpacking our moving boxes. She immediately asked me about my meeting with Cynthia. I explained to her all that was said and that if we say yes to this opportunity, we could be stationed in BO Sierra Leone in six months. I glanced over at Gayle and she was smiling.

I looked around at our new townhouse with boxes everywhere, and I see these three sons. I'm thinking, how am going to make sure I can provide for them? I know nothing about Africa.

This is crazy! My reluctance was getting the better of me and I was almost ready to call Cynthia the next morning to say thanks, but no thanks. But then Gayle took one look at me and noticed my worry and confusion. She asked, "What's wrong? Why do you look so worried?"

I said, "Honey, this was not in the plan. Maybe it's best we play it safe. We can think about this later in life. After all," I said, "I sent my resume off to Missouri for a civil rights job and we could hear something any day now. Maybe its best we stay put in the States."

Gayle says, "Delano, are you really pondering on whether or not we take advantage of this opportunity to go to Africa or one day go back to Missouri? I don't think there is any choice here, let's take a leap of faith and do this!"

This was a once in a lifetime opportunity and if I didn't do it now, chances were we would never have this opportunity again. After discussing this long into the night, we made a decision. It was settled. I would call Cynthia in the morning and tell her I would take the position.

The next morning I made the call and Cynthia welcomed it with great joy. Gayle was overjoyed with excitement and could not wait to get going. It was not long before we discovered that the BO Sierra Leone position was not available, but a position in Nigeria was. There was an Associate Director position opening in the Midwest region of the Peace Corps. This person would report to the Regional Director there and this would happen sooner rather than later. Gayle and I did our homework about Nigeria trying to learn as much as possible before our move. Things were moving so fast. This was actually somewhat of a blessing because we didn't have to finish unpacking, so we stopped and started repacking. We were going on a journey.

Before outgoing directors left for their posts, it was customary to meet with the Director of the Peace Corps. The first director was Sargent Shriver appointed by President John F. Kennedy. However, after President Kennedy's death, President Johnson asked Sargent Shriver to become the director of the Office of Economic Opportunity (OEO) and to assist in finding a replacement at the Peace Corps. With Shriver's blessing, LBJ appointed Jack Hood Vaughn to be the Director of the United States Peace Corps. As customary, I met with him before departing. He was a fairly small man with a well-groomed mustache. He stood about 5'7" and had been a former amateur and professional boxer. He also was a Marine Corps officer. He was very committed to the work the Peace Corps volunteers were doing around the world. I found him to be very approachable so I felt comfortable with him during our meeting.

There were two things he said that I will never forget. First, he said he was envious of me and that he would love to be traveling overseas and doing the job I was about to take on. He then said that the most important thing for me to do was to take time and soak it all up. He said to study the culture and the people and learn as much as I could about Africa. Finally, right before I left his office, he said that if I had any problems or any difficulties to contact him directly. This was very settling and comforting.

On June 24th 1966, I headed off to Nigeria with my family. We spent one night in New York and then boarded a plane the next day for Lagos, Nigeria. The plane stopped in Dakar Senegal, Roberts Field in Monrovia, Liberia, and Accra Ghana.

After sleeping some and dealing with the comfort of the kids, I knew we were getting close as I could feel the plane descending. It had been a long 12-hour flight with short stops along the way. I was excited and very nervous.

As we taxied on the runway and before the plane came to a stop, I remember watching from the window as the rolling stairs were being pushed out towards the door of the plane. Then the side door opened and the rolling stairs were locked into place.

Everyone deplaned and as we were doing so, I remember reaching the top of the stairs and was blinded by the glistening sun. I felt this massive rush of heat hit my face like never before. Wow! I had never felt heat like that. It was HOT!

Once we got into the Lagos airport, we were met by two Peace Corps staffers. This was comforting. They had information ready for us. They had information about our hotel arrangements where we would stay for one night and other orders and briefings ready to go. I was now on the job, a job in which I had no experience, in a country I knew nothing about. I trusted in my ability to lead through my communication skills hoping to make my family and all the people counting on me proud.

After getting settled in the Airport Hotel, we headed to the Country Director's house (my new boss), John McConnell. We had our first meal in Nigeria at the McConnell home, which started with a welcome Gin and Tonic.

As we were driving along to get there, I was just in awe of what I was seeing. There were all these people walking on the road and cars were honking their horns. I remember these huge trucks called *Lorries* carrying people. As I looked to the left out the car window, I could see goats roaming the roads. When I looked out the window to the right, the whole side of the road was lined with cattle. I was amazed watching people balance supplies on top of their heads while at the same time carrying bags of food. It was unreal and honestly, I was in culture shock.

I thought maybe I had bitten off more than I could chew. I wasn't sure if I could adapt because it was just so different from anything I had ever seen or done. I looked over at Gayle and she was smiling and pointing out the animals to the sons. She was taking it all in and couldn't have been more comfortable.

We arrived at the director's home. It was a large, lovely house and very comfortable. After we exchanged welcome hugs and smiles, we were offered cold refreshing drinks. The Peace Corps Director for Nigeria, John McConnell, was very welcoming. We ate dinner prepared for us, had drinks, and we talked about my assignment as the

Associate Director of the Peace Corps in Benin City, Nigeria. I was told that I would be leading about 160 volunteers, mostly teachers, with some being community development volunteers.

I became very eager to get started. After one night in Lagos, we took a short flight to Benin City. When we arrived at the Benin City Airport, it hit me; I knew I was not in Kansas anymore.

June 25th, 1966 - *"Ladies and gentlemen, this is your captain speaking. Welcome to Benin City, Nigeria. The local time is 3:00 p.m. Thank you for flying Nigeria Airways.*

Two Peace Corps staffers, as well as Mike Taylor the Peace Corps doctor and his wife, Joyce, met us. They were expecting us and excited to take us to the lovely home they had secured for our family. It was a modern house newly built out of concrete block.

We arrived at the house and it was beautiful inside. The living room area was large and it had an up-to-date kitchen. It felt and looked warm and homey. We went to the master bedroom. It was a huge, beautiful room with a nice, big bed, but hanging from the ceiling above the bed was a mosquito net covering all of its sides. That's when reality set in.

Yep, we were in the bush where malaria-carrying mosquitoes were rampant. We had been briefed about this in the States, but the briefing paled compared to the reality that hit us in the face. Every seven days, we took our malaria medicine, *Chloroquine,* and you can bet that we made sure our boys also took theirs.

Benin City was filled with life and culture, it was tropical-rainforest. It was very hot but cooled off at night during the *Harmattan* months usually between the end of November and the middle of March. Almost all roads in Benin were dirt. The main road, which led in and out of the government reservation where we lived, was partially paved, but other roads in the city were undeveloped. The only paved road was the road from the central roundabout leading out toward Lagos.

As time went on, I began to adapt and understand Nigeria and its culture. I was proud of the Peace Corps volunteers. Not only did we drink lots of Star beer and dance the "highlife," the Peace Cops made a difference in the lives of the

Nigerian students and in the communities where we served.

There are times even now that I wonder just how I did it. One thing is for certain, it would have never happened without taking my leap of faith.

A VERY SCARY MOMENT
IN GULU, UGANDA

> **"The Peace Corps is guilty of enthusiasm and a crusading spirit, but we're not apologetic about it."**
>
> - *Sargent Shriver*

In October 1967, we moved to Kampala Uganda from Benin City, Nigeria. The Peace Corps program in Nigeria was suspended due to the Nigerian civil war and we were evacuated from that country. After the evacuation in the summer of 1967, I was offered the position of Peace Corps Director in Uganda. In February 1968, our fourth child, Phillip, was born Kampala.

The position of Country Director was a promotion and it came with more responsibility, and more volunteers to assist, observe and serve. I was in my element for sure.

The United States. Ambassador to Uganda was Henry Stebbins, a career and very well respected diplomat. He and his wife, Barbara, were lovely people and very caring. Barbara Stebbins was very involved in developing support systems for treating the local people of Uganda who suffered from the eye disease *Trachoma*. She encouraged the United States Peace Corps to develop a Peace Corps program designed to train volunteers to treat Trachoma eye disease in Uganda. Peace Corps Washington approved this program and there were about 20 volunteers who worked on Trachoma eye disease. This was just one of the programs that volunteers took on and I oversaw as Director of the Peace Corps. In Uganda, there were more than 150 volunteers in Education.

The Contractors Overseas Representative, (C.O.R) was Sal Messina. Sal's job was assisting the volunteers in teaching methods and helping them to develop their curricula and formatting their syllabi. He enjoyed his job and loved interacting with the volunteers in the field.

Part of the Peace Corps Director's job is to spend two or three days at a time in the field to support the volunteers. This meant that I would often travel with Sal and we would ride together, usually in a CJ6 Jeep because they were great for getting in and out of bad roads and swamp areas.

Late one afternoon, I got word at the Peace Corps office that I was needed to visit volunteers in Gulu, a city north of Kampala. It should be noted that Gulu was the home of Idi Amin, and this could provoke challenges to anyone living or visiting there. We were very aware of Idi Amin and his infatuation with power and control as General in charge of the Army in Uganda so we knew to be careful. Consequently, we knew better than to make the trip by road that late in the day leading into night. Sal Messina also needed to visit volunteers in Gulu so Sal and I agreed to make the trip together. He said that he would be by to pick me up the following morning

The next day arrived and off we went. I told Gayle I would see her and the kids in about three days and that this was a normal field visit. When Sal and I got to Gulu, all was quiet. We met with several volunteers and they were glad to see us. Later that day, we left one of the volunteer posts and headed back out into the field to visit some schools. It had been a long day and it was hot.

Most roads in Uganda were murram roads which are unpaved with a gravel surface. They are very patchy so one had to pay careful attention while driving. We were just beginning our trip back with Sal was driving, when I felt the Jeep shake and then we began to swerve.

At that exact moment I didn't know what was happening. I looked over to Sal trying his best to navigate the Jeep back onto the smooth part of the road. Then again there was another big swerve and another huge bump. At this point I knew that we were headed for possible trouble. Sal was focused on the road with both hands on the wheel. Sweat was pouring from both of our foreheads. And then it happened, I could feel the Jeep going off balance and we were headed for a crash.

I looked to the right of me and saw only dirt and a cliff so I hoped that if we flipped, it would be to the left. Just seconds later, we were headed for a big tumble. I did all I could and braced myself for what could be a serious flip. Sal and I both knew the Jeep was out of control and, unfortunately, it flipped to the right. I fell out, landed on the left side of my body, then rolled down the cliff. Thank goodness the Jeep didn't roll over me. After that moment, total blackness, I was out, unconscious.

I woke up in a Grade C hospital lying on a very uncomfortable cot. I was hot, thirsty and my left arm was throbbing in a sling. Now, let me explain what kind of hospital this was. In a Grade C or lower, this meant that a local doctor would come and see you and administer to you, but there was no food and nothing to drink. In these hospitals, you depended on your family to provide all your nourishment. As I came to, I asked about Sal, but no one there, knew who or where he was.

I tried to communicate with people to get answers. I believe that Sal, who had been taken to the local "catering rest house" was able to call back to Peace Corps Kampala to inform them of the accident and to ask for help. The Peace Corps doctor after having been notified of the accident, called the hospital in Gulu and was able to speak with me. He told me not to accept any medications or vaccines. I understood. I just wanted to get out of there. The Peace Corps doctor informed the hospital staff that I was one of the highest ranking Americans in Uganda and that I reported directly to the American Ambassador. He asked that I be treated well. Eventually, Sal was able to bring me some food and drink from the Catering Rest House.

Looking back, I feel very fortunate. There was so much that could have happened and it could have ended up much worse. Once we got back to Kampala, I had my arm examined at Mulago Hospital where they took excellent care of me. I was told that the head of the radius bone in the arm had been smashed so I had minor surgery to repair it and several weeks later I was as good as new. I have to tell you, the whole experience was scary!

MARION BARRY
HOW WE MET

> **"Leadership has a harder job to do than just choose sides. It must bring sides together."**
>
> *- Jesse Jackson*

During my 35 years in Washington DC, I had the great fortune to meet and get to know many people who influenced my life. Washington is a powerful city and with power comes conflict. DC has its share of naysayers, backstabbers and self-centered individuals out for their own political gain. Therefore, it was important for me to form good, honest friendships which could withstand the daily rhetoric of Washington politics.

Marion Barry was a friend, a confidant and a leader. Although he was often criticized for his demons that eventually got the best of him, deep down he was a great visionary and fantastic politician. Marion had an amazing ability to bring all types of different people together. He viewed the city of Washington as a model for others. He was always one step ahead of his critics, as he spoke with authority, promise and passion.

Washington DC was in great hands. Marion Barry was no stranger to poverty or the struggle for civil rights. He believed in helping the poor and giving all people of all classes an opportunity to succeed. He was approachable and had charm and presence. For years, I studied and watched Marion and admired him from a distance. I was fascinated not just by his ability to speak up for what he believed in, but for having the courage to make needed changes. He was a master at connecting the dots.

In 1971 when I was working for Senator Edward Brooke, I learned and came to understand how the United States Senate worked. I could navigate my way around the Senate very well, but I was not as familiar with the workings of the US House of Representatives. It was in this year, 1971, that the citizens of Washington DC were able to elect a representative to the House of Representatives. Reverend Walter E. Fauntroy was elected as the Non-Voting Delegate to the U.S. House of Representatives.

Walter Fauntroy was an activist and civil rights pioneer. He, along with Jessie Jackson and Andrew Young, were very instrumental in writing many speeches for Dr. Martin Luther King Jr. Fauntroy, like King, Jackson and Young, were all Baptist ministers. While traveling with Dr. King during marches and demonstrations for equal rights, Fauntroy assisted in organizing the March on Washington in 1963.

In 1970, Congress passed the District of Columbia Delegate Act authorizing the election of a Non-Voting Delegate to the House of Representatives. Reverend Walter Fauntroy, a confidant of Dr. King and an activist in civil rights, ran in a crowded field for the Non-Delegate position. Fauntroy campaigned on a platform of Home Rule for Washington DC and ending job discrimination.

In a field of six candidates, Rev. Fauntroy won the primary with over 44% of the vote. In the general election in March 1971, Rev. Fauntroy easily won and became the first Non-Voting Delegate to the House of Representatives in 100 years.

Like most big political news in DC, word got around that Fauntroy was looking for a chief of staff. This interested me. I knew it was an opportunity to get closer to the real political change taking place in the city and I wanted to be involved. I sent my resume to Rev. Fauntroy, hoping to get an interview. Early on I had learned, nothing is wrong with searching for new opportunities for advancement.

After a couple weeks, I heard from Fauntroy himself and landed an interview. I was ready, I was prepared and I was sure my resume would speak for itself. I remember arriving at the Longworth House Office building and locating Fauntroy's office. It was mid-morning and he greeted me with a soft handshake. I wasn't sure what that meant, but I got the feeling he wanted this interview to be over with. I took a quick glance at him before sitting and was amazed at how short he was. He was a little man, not over 140 pounds I'd say, and dressed in a nice blue suit and matching vest.

We spent about an hour together discussing the job and my resume. Again, I just got the feeling it was not going well. There was just something about him that made me think he was not at all interested in hiring me. But I stayed the course and tried not to become distracted. I continued to confidently answer all his questions.

Then, from out of nowhere, he says, "Del, before I make my decision, I need you to talk to three people." I shook my head with a confused nod.

I said, "Congressman, that's fine with me." Then, I asked, "Who would you like me to meet with and when?"

He said, "First, I would like you to speak with a good friend of mine, John Hechinger. I need you to get to know him. Then I want you to meet Jim Gibson, another close friend of mine. He's quite bright, very well thought of, and I value his opinion." The congressman then said, "And lastly, Del, I need you to meet with DC activist and leader, Marion Barry. He has an organization called PRIDE. I think it would be good for you to talk to him." So I wasted no time and immediately contacted and set up meetings with all three men.

John Hechinger was the owner of The Hechinger Company, a family owned hardware and lumber company that started in 1911. He had several locations throughout the DC area, was wealthy and very active in DC Democratic politics. John was a tall, slender man. He was a soft-spoken man with a great sense of humor. There was a very kind and gentle way about him. I liked him as soon as we met and we immediately hit it off. We had a great conversation filled with politics, family and the Chief of Staff position for Delegate Fauntroy.

As we concluded our visit, John said, "Walter and I are old friends. We go back quite a way. Of course I can't hire you, but I'm certainly going to let Walter know that I think you would do a great job." I was pleased.

Next up was Jim Gibson who worked with the Urban Institute, a grass roots organization in Washington. When I arrived at our meeting he appeared to be just as he had been described, a very intellectual and savvy person. I wasn't sure that I connected with him, everything seemed sort of neutral.

Finally, I was scheduled to meet with Marion Barry. In my mind, I knew that I had to at least hit it off with two out of the three to even have a chance of getting the job. So I decided that I would not risk leaving anything to chance and did research about Marion. He was a very smart and educated man with a bachelor's degree from Fisk University and I also discovered that he had been accepted and attended the University of Kansas to obtain his master's degree in chemistry. This was a great bit of information. Kansas is my alma mater. I knew I could use this to help make a connection.

So the day came and I met with Marion. Feeling confident in my suit and skinny tie, I was well prepared for questions that might come my way. As I walked into his office at PRIDE, Marion greeted me, dressed in an African dashiki. Without a doubt, this would be an interesting meeting. I reached out, shook his hand, and immediately cut to my icebreaker. I said, "Marion, I heard that you received a scholarship at the University of Kansas to study for your master's degree in chemistry. I graduated from KU in '60."

He gave me a quick glance and a curious stare. I was actually a bit intimidated. Marion stood about 6'2" and had a football player type build. I wasn't sure if I had said something inaccurate or not.

He then said, "Del, how do you know about that?" with very curious eyes and somewhat frustrated grin. Before I could answer, he says, "Well, let me just say that I was at the KU campus in Lawrence for one semester and had to get out of that town." He continued to say that the town seemed slow and offered little for him so he left.

At that moment, I knew I had touched a nerve. It was almost as if he wanted no one to know he was highly educated. I found this very interesting. Here is a bright African American man running his own organization to help educate, form and shape other blacks in the city, but didn't want them to know his educational background. I didn't press the issue and quickly moved on with our interview.

After several questions, I could tell Marion took a liking to me. We were roughly the same age. Marion may have been a year older than I. He could see I had passion and the real connection came when I talked about my experience in Africa. I could see that Marion was close to his roots and the fact that I had lived and experienced the "motherland" firsthand was very intriguing to him.

I also believed that he admired my ability to lead and that I took great pride in my education.

We continued to talk for about an hour and what started out a little shaky turned out to be an excellent exchange.

I left the meeting with Marion feeling as though I would get high recommendations from both Hechinger and Marion. I felt these recommendations would be enough to compel Fauntroy to make me his new Chief of Staff. And sure enough, just days later, I got a call from Walter Fauntroy with an offer of the job as Chief of Staff. I learned that I had earned the support of all three men. I gladly accepted and was excited to begin another phase in my political career. It turned out to be just the beginning.

TRANSITION MAGICIAN

In 1973, I moved from the Federal government to the private sector. I took a job with Chesapeake and Potomac Telephone Company as their Public Affairs Manager. This was a great opportunity for growth and a getaway from the hustle of government and politics, I thought.

It was not long before I got the itch to get involved again, this time by way of running for city council in 1974. My superiors at the phone company were very gracious in letting me pursue this election without the fear of losing my job if I didn't succeed. At this time, there were two "at large" seats up for grabs in the Democratic Party primary.

The Home Rule bill provided for minority party representation in the "at-large" races by stipulating that the majority party, Democratic, could hold no more than two seats. The other two seats would be filled by candidates from the minority parties, Republican, Independent and Statehood. I had some name recognition in the city, but not as much as others running.

Once I got my campaign organized, it was brought to my attention early on that Marion Barry would be the one candidate sure to be elected for one "at-large" seat. This meant there was only one other seat that I might be able to grab. I was sure that I didn't have the political power to beat Marion, but I felt certain I could grab the other seat.

After a long and hard fight, I lost. I came in third. Marion was elected for one seat and the Reverend Douglas Moore came in second and was elected to the other seat. There were nine of us running in the Democratic Party primary. Although I didn't win, coming in third was a real good showing. In fact, there were only a few thousand votes separating me from the winner, Reverend Douglas Moore.

So after the loss, I refocused my efforts on my job at C&P Telephone Company. I knew I could learn a lot and there was room for advancement. I was in a good place professionally, but wouldn't you know it, once I got comfortable, temptation came calling again.

It happened in 1976. I was progressing at C&P Telephone and had been promoted to an

Assistant Vice President. I was becoming a rising star. No other African American had advanced as far and as fast as I had. It had been a wild ride up the ladder. I had great mentors guiding me and trusting me while they taught me everything about the business. I was very fortunate and very blessed.

But then, early on a Monday morning, I got a call from Marion Barry and he says, "Del, I think you should run for the City Council again. There are seats available and I know you can win easily. This will give us a chance to work together and change the city." He and I had kept in touch after my loss two years prior and we became close.

Wow, I thought, this is not what I need to hear. In my selfish mind, this was the opportunity of a lifetime. However, my wife, Gayle, was very put off by the political process that took place in '74. She was very disturbed by the corrupt and self-serving nature that politics played. She would not raise a family in what she felt was an unhealthy environment. She was so adamant about this that she said if I ran for political office again, she would divorce me and I believed her.

I said Marion, "I am flattered, but this is just not going to happen." I explained Gayle's position on politics and he understood. I told him I was in his corner and to keep making good changes for the city. He was appreciative and we left it at that.

On March 9, 1977, Washington DC was frozen in fear. Three buildings downtown had been taken over by a group of Hanafi Muslims led by Hammas Abdul Khaalis whose family had been murdered in 1973. Their demand was for an apology for the murders. They also demanded that the movie *Mohammad, Messenger of God* be removed from local theaters. Over 100 hostages were held. This was one of the most bizarre situations to happen in the nation's capital.

Later that day it was reported that when the Hanafi Muslims invaded the District Building where the Mayor and City Council convene, they shot and killed one young man and wounded several others. One of the wounded was Marion Barry. He was later taken to a nearby hospital where he was treated. After a day and a half of this act of terrorism, the FBI and DC Police brought the situation under control and all hostages were released.

Shortly thereafter, I talked with Marion and he said he was fine and wanted to get back to work. He was always concerned about the people of the city. He felt a sense of responsibility to the people. He felt that the city council position he held just wasn't powerful enough to make the much needed changes he envisioned.

So in 1978, I got another very important call from Marion. I was at my office at C&P when my personal line rang. It was Marion. He said, "Del, can I come by to see you this morning?"

I said, "Marion, I'm busy, why such short notice?" He says it's important and will take only thirty minutes. I said fine and I found thirty minutes in my schedule to meet him.

He arrived right on time and sat down in my office. He said, "Del, I've decided to run for mayor."

I said, "Mayor? Marion, you just got on the council. Don't you think this is a bit soon?"

He said, "No (with a strong desire in his voice), I need to lead this city in the right direction. I know I can do it and the time is now."

I said, "Marion, are you sure?"

He responded, "Del, I was shot last year by the Hanafi Muslims. Who knows if I'll be around to run in ten years?"

We both chuckled and I then asked, "What can I do to help?"

He said, "Del, I need your connections both in the public and private sectors. You are very well thought of and I believe with your endorsement and energy, I know I can win this thing." I thought for a moment, making sure I was not overstepping my promise to Gayle, and I then agreed to help.

Marion left my office that day with a big smile as if he had landed a big fish. The truth was, Marion was a very smart and calculating politician. I admired his political tenacity and his courage to be out front.

My endorsement to him meant more than the naked eye could see. But Marion got it. He understood that I connected with Ward 3 and that he needed this area of the city to win the election.

Ward 3 was an upper middle-class area of Northwest Washington DC. The population was predominantly white. I lived with my family in Ward 3. Marion understood that I was well respected and could be trusted. He also knew that I had political and social connections to Blacks, Whites, Jews and Catholics in Ward 3 and across the city. He believed that if I supported him for mayor, then others would follow.

I hit the ground running, working so hard for Marion that I one day my boss called me into his office for a little chat. My boss and mentor, Ralph Frey, wanted to talk about my being so public in endorsing a political candidate.

He said, "Del, as business executives in the private sector, we serve all people – Republicans, Democrats and Independents. You can't be so vocal about *your* choice. It's not the prudent thing to do I suggest you tone it down."

I took his words to heart and worked for Marion only in my spare time, but I was committed. I knew he was the best man for the job. I knew his vision and he had an incredible knack for politics. No one was more equipped to take the city further than Marion. But it came with a risk for me as a businessman.

Marion was running against the incumbent mayor, Walter Washington, and a very viable opponent, Sterling Tucker. Sterling was a seasoned politician who was serving as City Council chairman and was well respected. It would be a tough race. The risk was that if Marion lost, the company could possibly be out of political favor with the new mayor.

I took the risk and it paid off! Marion won and became Mayor of Washington DC in 1978. It was an amazing time for both of us. I will never forget what he told me at the victory party right before he made his speech. He leaned over and whispered in my ear, "Your stock in the Telephone Company will be high now." And boy was he right!

The next day when I returned to the office at C&P Telephone, my boss Ralph Frey greeted me saying, "Mr. Lewis, may I get you a cup of coffee?" We both laughed. Ralph Frey knew that I didn't drink coffee. He did know, however, that the future was bright for the city and the phone company.

Two weeks went by and Marion contacted me again. He thanked me for all my hard work and then he asked for another huge favor. "Del, I really need your help in putting my government together. I need your connections in helping me fill each position in my administration so we can accomplish all the things that are in my plan for the city."

I said, "Sure, Marion. How would you like to proceed?"

He said, "Well, I am now the Mayor and this is now official city business. I would need you to take a paid leave from C&P for a month to six weeks and help make this happen. I suggest you draft a letter to your boss outlining that I am asking for your services and that they compensate you while you are on leave. Then send me the letter and I will sign it and send it to your boss."

I said, "Great."

Days later, my boss, Mr. Frey, called me into his office and said that he had received a letter from the Mayor requesting my help in the transition of the city government. Now this was rather funny because I could have recited the letter word for word since I drafted it.

Anyway, Mr. Frey said, "I think this is a must for you to do, Del, and we need to respond immediately. Why don't you draft a letter to the Mayor outlining that we will gladly pay for your services for however long it takes to help him transition his government."

Now this is getting funnier so I chuckle to myself and do as he said. I draft a second letter to the Mayor and off I went.

I spent several weeks helping the Mayor assemble an incredible team. We infused his cabinet with smart, young, enthusiastic and forward-thinking people. It was an exciting responsibility. The cabinet was such a hit that it even made the front page headline of the Washington Post. I will never forget what it read –

"Delano Lewis, Mayor Barry's Transition Magician!"

What an honor!

"LADIES AND GENTLEMEN, THE VICE PRESIDENT OF THE UNITED STATES"

> **"If you're walking down the right path and you're willing to keep walking, eventually you'll make progress."**
> - *President Barack Obama*

In March 2014, Gayle I were visiting our son, Brian, in Florida. We were there to relax, enjoy the sunshine and visit with the grandkids.

One evening after eating too much pizza and having great conversation, Brian asked if we had ever seen the HBO movie *Game Change*. When we said no, he said, "Oh, it's a must see, I think you will find it fascinating."

The movie is a great story about how someone with little recognition one day could then be vaulted to the very top in politics in a matter of moments. I got a little chill on my skin. Something was hitting home in that exact moment. I continued to watch the movie with great intensity, trying sometimes to keep my ego in check and my mind from slipping into the *what ifs* of the past. Let me explain.

It was 1988 and I was an executive at Chesapeake and Potomac Telephone Company, one of the largest private employers in the greater Washington DC metropolitan area. My notoriety was rising both in the public and private sectors.

Early in my career at the phone company, I became a very active member of *The Greater Washington Board of Trade*. This was the largest business organization in the metropolitan area. I was involved with several committees on the board and used this organization to network personally and professionally to build relationships.

I eventually became the President of the Metropolitan Washington DC Board of Trade. It is a prestigious and very influential organization. The members of the Board of Trade were movers and shakers in the Washington DC business world.

I got to know a businessman, Herb Miller, who was the President and CEO of Western Development Company. Herb put together investment groups to buy land and develop property. His firm at the time was in Georgetown, a prestigious and historical area of Washington DC.

One day, Herb asked me if I would like to be involved with a development project called "Georgetown Park." It would be a mixed-use development of restaurants and shops in Georgetown.

Herb explained that he was putting together a group of people he thought would be interested in the project and could add value. I knew Herb was a visionary and this seemed to be a good business move.

One of the other investors in Herb's group was Bob Mendelsohn. Bob was originally from San Francisco where he was a member of the Board of San Francisco Supervisors. I knew little about this board but what I could gather; it was a very influential board functioning very much like a city council.

I got to know Bob as a person with great insight and vision. He now resided full time in DC and knew of the power and political structure of the nation's capital. He also knew of my political connections and my relationship with the mayor, Marion Barry. Everyone knew that if you were a developer and wanted to see change in the city, it was very helpful to have a good and close relationship with the mayor. This was my calling card and everyone knew it.

After some time, Bob Mendelsohn asked me to lunch to discuss a political idea. I agreed and we met for lunch. As we sat over lunch, Bob, who pulls no punches, began with an absolute bomb of an opener.

He said, "Del, I have been watching you and how you operate, both professionally and politically. I'm very impressed with your skills to communicate with people and to lead. I see how people listen when you speak and this quality needs to be put onto a bigger stage." He continued, "Del, I know how you can become Vice President of the United States."

Well, when I got up from the floor after falling from my chair, I said, "Bob, what are you talking about? How can that happen?"

Bob revealed his plan. He began by saying I should eventually run for Mayor of Washington

DC. He didn't think that I should run against Marion. He suggested that maybe after Marion's second term, he would not run again and I should run.

Bob continued, "Del, I know you will win and you will do a great job as Mayor of Washington, DC." He went on to explain that Washington, being our nation's capital, had the eyes of every state watching its every move and this included local city politics. He was correct. There is no other city where the Mayor makes front-page news in every major paper around the country.

He explained that once I became Mayor, all eyes in the country would be on me. My name would surface in political conversations. News reports and papers from around the country would hedge their bets on the next rising star in politics and my name would be in the mix.

He said, "Del, this is how it works. You land a high profile job in politics, like becoming Mayor. You do a great job and earn the support of your constituents. You run as a Democrat and all the movers and shakers of the Democratic Party will begin to take notice. Then you run for a position on the National Democratic Committee and heads will start turning and your name will start to reverberate as a viable candidate for the highest office. I believe this is when your name could surface as a candidate for Vice President."

I was flattered and amazed at how he connected the dots. At first, I wasn't really buying into it, but after much thought; I could see the reality of this taking place. Once I removed my ego, it was easy for me to acknowledge that his plan had some merit.

I did not talk to too many people about this. I shared our meeting with two close friends and told Gayle about it, but that was it. I never put the plan into action. But looking back now, I believe Bob was precisely right on.

When I study the rise of President Obama and how he splashed onto the national political scene, it is eerie how similar the process was to what I had been told to do 20 years prior.

Do I have any regrets? The answer is no. Everything happens for a reason. I will always have a desire to dream big and to lead large.

CITY LIFE
3236 McKINLEY STREET

> **"Nothing I've ever done has given me more joy and rewards than being a father to my children."**
>
> *- Delano E. Lewis, Sr.*

We returned from Uganda in 1969. We had four sons each one with his own personality. They thought differently and learned differently and spoke their minds in their own unique ways.

As for me, there were days when I wasn't sure if I was being the best dad I could be. Sometimes this bothered me. I was an only child without the experience of growing up with siblings. My father was not consistently present in my growing up. He worked on the railroad and was gone from home quite a lot. I knew that I was on my own in the "dad department."

In 1972, we made our first home purchase. It was at 3236 McKinley Street in northwest Washington DC. The neighborhood was known as

Chevy Chase, DC, not to be confused with Chevy Chase, Maryland, which was adjacent. Chevy Chase DC was a wonderful neighborhood filled with many families and lots of kids. There were several parks and playgrounds that the kids could walk to and plenty of activities going on in the streets and back alleys. It was safe and very friendly.

The neighborhood was filled with hard working, middle-class families of various religions and ethnic backgrounds. We were one of the few Black families in the neighborhood. Our family and the other families developed sustaining close friendships over the years.

This house and neighborhood is where our sons grew up. Living in Chevy Chase, DC was a learning experience for me since I grew up in an all Black neighborhood. I had to reconcile my childhood environment growing up with what my children were experiencing now. I knew this experience would be critical to their understanding of people living together who were from varied races and backgrounds.

We were a family grounded in faith and values. Gayle and I had basic principles we both agreed on before we had children. We firmly believed in structure and communication and never hitting our children. We taught our kids there were consequences for their actions. I knew I wanted to be a father who showed his love. I believed in hugs and kisses and telling my children I loved them. I also believed in celebrations and acknowledgements for a job well done.

Early on, when the kids were still young, I started my first dad tradition. It was simple and was always received with great enthusiasm. Each night I would try to arrive home by 6:45 p.m. because I knew that our family dinner at 7:00 p.m. was important. The kids knew what time I would get home each day and would always be close to the front door waiting to hear the screen door open. They knew then that daddy was home. I could hear them yelling as I opened the front door, "Daddy's home, daddy's home." As loving and exciting as this would seem, the sons were actually more focused on the several packs of M&M's I would have in my pockets every night.

As the sons grew older, I knew that it was important for me to take an even more visible role of "dad" in the household. I knew that it was important for each boy to believe in himself and not be afraid to speak his mind. We had no one size fits all agenda in our house. If you had an opinion, a question, or a thought, then it was yours to share and it was valued. This was never more evident than the incredible atmosphere we created at the dinner table.

One day, Gayle and I decided that it may be a good idea to have assigned seats at the table. However, we did not want to sit at the head and the foot. The table should be democratic and everyone should be equally treated. If I sat at the head of the table, this may appear to be too authoritarian, making the sons feel that their opinions may not be valued. At the time, I didn't realize the impact these dinners would have in the future of our family or the extreme importance of encouraging open communication. The table discussion was open to everyone to bring up whatever issues were on their minds. We would take turns and go around the table. There was never a night that someone did not participate. It was incredible.

Phill, being the youngest and also the shortest in height, often would not sit in his chosen seat at the end of the table. He would stand. We felt this was his right. If standing made him feel more comfortable and important, then we encouraged it.

Del, Jr., the oldest, was always very direct in his thoughts and always got his point across. Geoff, the second child, was always figuring out a way to infuse his viewpoint, often with examples, great persistence and repetition. Brian was the analytical child, always trying to find a hole in someone's theory or story and consistently wanting to know 'why.' Gayle and I would often sit back and listen with great pride. There were many nights where we would have to play referee, but it was always a great learning experience.

One summer evening as we were having dinner, I had a thought about taking a weekend family trip. I was immediately met with resistance from the sons. I did my best to convince them this would be fun, but to no avail. I must admit that I was upset about the sons not wanting to do something together as a family. Maybe they were just getting older and had other interests but it didn't matter. I knew that family time, even for a day trip, was good quality time and would be a good experience.

I let the idea go for a while and brought it up again at a later dinner conversation. Again, I was met with boos and a myriad of excuses. I was upset and needed to find an answer. And then it hit me, why not force the sons to go. This did not set too well with Gayle and she asked me if this idea of forcing the sons was really worth it. I responded yes and held strong to my position.

The next family dinner would change the landscape of our family forever and what happened still carries on within the families of all of our sons and now our grandkids. After prayer at the dinner table on a Saturday evening, I told everyone that they needed to be up in the morning, dressed, and at the front door by 8:00 a.m. sharp. Again, I was met by massive resistance. There was a mutiny going on at the table, questions flying from five directions (yes, Gayle included). What was I thinking?

Finally, I said, "There is no discussion on this matter." That was the night the dinner table went quiet. I needed to break the ice, so I said, "Listen, I promise that this will be fun." I assured everyone this was not a punishment and that I had given this activity great thought. I eventually clinched approval from the sons when I said it would not involve going to church on that Sunday and they should wear jeans, shorts or anything comfortable. I finished my speech by telling everyone this was the first official FFF (Three F) event.

Everyone just looked at me and said, "Dad, what in God's name is Three F?"

I said, "It stands for Forced Family Fun!" Their eyes rolled and the funny looks continued. My plan was now in action.

The next morning arrived and we all gathered at the front door. A couple of sons tried to pry information from me about our destination. My lips were sealed. I had told Gayle, but she was quiet as a mouse.

By 9:00 a.m. we had everyone in the car and took off. We were barely two miles from home when the questions began. "When are we going to be there? How long is the ride? How much further?"

I reacted calmly with answers that promised fun and a good time. We interacted with each other in the car by telling jokes and playing games. Phill was always good for a joke or two that kept us all in stitches. After about two hours on the road all became quiet in the car. Most everyone had nodded off even as we were getting closer to my first FFF activity.

Del woke up just in time to see and read aloud the big blue highway sign: *Welcome to Pennsylvania.* Then they all woke up and I knew that I could not keep this surprise from them much longer. They were all very curious about why we had come to Pennsylvania. I wasn't sure if I could keep the surprise from them much longer. As we got closer to my surprise destination there was another sign that read, *Hershey, Pennsylvania, 5 miles.* Now the questions were coming at me from all directions. I knew I needed to give in.

Then out of nowhere, there it was, a huge banner sign draped thirty feet in the sky above two large black gates. It read, *Hershey Park, Pennsylvania.* We were here, we made it. I stopped the car and said to the sons, "Look guys, we made it to a great amusement park." They were all excited and I was feeling like Dad of the Year. This FFF plan had paid off and I was now a hero.

We approached the entrance, pulled up to the closed gate and there we saw one guard. He was looking at us like we were half crazy. I rolled down my window and asked him, "What time does the park open?" He just gave me a blank look and pointed to a big sign on the gates in front of us. It read, "*Sorry, the Park is Closed Today.*" I asked, "Is the park normally closed on Sunday?" He replied, "No, but it is today."

As I turned the car around and we pulled away from the closed gate, I was feeling dejected and somewhat of a failure. The sons were all excited to go to an amusement park and it was closed. I could tell this would be a long ride home. We searched for some fast food hoping that some full bellies would erase the magnitude of my faux pas, but it seemed as though nothing in the town was open and so we headed back home.

To my surprise, the conversation and attitude in the car as we drove home was rather upbeat. We didn't get into the park, but there was something bigger accomplished - we shared family togetherness and the understanding that not all things work out as planned.

Today, the Lewis Family and the extended Lewis Families all have various forms of FFF. We even started a very competitive, but fun, NFL football pool appropriately named *Forced Family Football*. The pool has existed since 1996.

Sharing this memory invites you into some of my most delicate moments of fatherhood. I've never had all the answers and most of the time I was just going on instinct.

As I mentioned before, I had no great road map to learn from growing up. I was an only child and had no sense of what it is like to have siblings. This was all an incredible learning experience for me.

I believe with all of my heart and soul the one thing that made our family unit prosper was the ability to communicate. I learned so much from just listening to them talk and express themselves. I have always said family is the most important part of my existence. I thank God to this day for Forced Family Fun!

Many years later, I learned from a fellow board member of Eastman Kodak, who was also President of the Hershey Company, that Hershey Park is closed only one day out of the year for cleaning and general maintenance. Can you believe, I chose that day for our first Three F activity?

SUBURBAN LIFE
MOVING TO
POTOMAC, MARYLAND

> **"Human beings are the only creatures on earth who allow their children to come back home."**
>
> *- Anonymous*

I have always been a planner. Ever since I can remember, I have mapped out my every day. I grew up with the ability to map out a plan in my mind and then put it to paper. I would then study my notes and fine-tune my outline. Once satisfied, I would put my plan into action.

Truth be told, this simple system has rarely let me down. Time after time, I would see my idea on paper and execute. Growing up in a segregated world and not having many choices for college and law school, it was very important for me to learn how not to fail. Hard work and attention to detail was the key. I tried not to leave any stone unturned and to think of all the obstacles that might derail me. I was always a forward thinker and understood the basic principle, practice makes perfect.

If I had a nickel for every legal yellow pad I have filled out with notes, ideas, business plans, homework, board meetings, new and interesting thoughts, family matters and so on, I would be beyond wealthy. To this day, a good pen and a legal pad give me great comfort in mapping out a road to victory.

For years, my sons watched me doodle on yellow pads and would look at me quizzically. I would try to explain to them that organizing my thoughts on paper allowed me to visualize them later. It was my way of keeping all of my running thoughts and questions in front of me. It also taught me about the power of visualization. I understood that if I could see my thoughts on paper, then I could actualize them.

By 1982, family dinners with all six of us were becoming less frequent. As the sons were getting older, they were getting involved in their own activities. Del, Jr. was graduating from college soon and Geoff and Brian were recently out of high school. Phill was in school, honing his acting career. However, on this night, we all were home at the dinner table.

Gayle and I had been talking about possibly moving to another house and just didn't know where, when or even what it should look like. After dinner, while still sitting around the table, the conversation turned to the usual sports or the brothers ribbing each other about one thing or another. I spoke-up saying "I have a topic up for discussion".

With everybody's attention, I reached behind my chair and on a small table was my yellow pad. I could see the look on the sons' faces as they knew this conversation was about to get real boring, real fast. I didn't let it bother me knowing that what I was about to propose would be of interest to everyone.

I looked at everyone at the table and said, "If we move to another house, what would be the perfect house for you?" There was a moment of silence before the banter began. I took control quickly and went around the table. The input was incredible.

The room was abuzz with such suggestions as a swimming pool, a tennis court, a large enough yard to throw a party. There were several mentions of everyone having his own bedroom and plenty of bathrooms. Gayle chimed in for a nice big kitchen and dining area. I thought it would be great to have a huge patio with a BBQ pit and nice big yard for family gatherings. Del wanted, above all, to have a circular driveway.

It was a great conversation that just kept getting more exciting as the night went on. The whole time I'm taking notes on my yellow pad. I knew these were all dreams and desires and that if we could find something with maybe half of these requests then we would have succeeded.

Months passed by and the kids went back to their various activities. Gayle and I looked for possible new homes. We never shared our vision with anyone except the family. This was *our* wish list. It was important to dream, but to also be realistic on what we could afford.

Then one day it happened. We found the perfect house in Potomac, Maryland, about forty minutes from where we were living in DC. It was hard to say goodbye to our amazing neighborhood where the sons grew up. Gayle and I had made such good friends with so many people and they would be missed. But we let everyone know that we were less than an hour away and we had plenty of room.

The house we found was on five acres of land, had a swimming pool and had plenty of room to build a tennis court if we wanted. It had seven bedrooms and five baths. There was a huge kitchen and a circular driveway. It was everything and more I had put down on paper. This memory has so many little pieces to it I just had to share.

First, I wanted to point out the power of planning. My kids still laugh at me to this day when I pull out the legal pad. They know it's time for the conversation to get serious, but I think they now appreciate proper planning and note taking.

Second, I have always believed in dreaming. I was raised by a mother who thought the world of me and instilled in me from a very young age that I could do anything, except sing.

By asking all the sons that night what their dream was for a new house, it allowed us all as a family to dream together. We never doubted our resolve and sure enough, the house became a reality. This was an amazing family dream come true.

NATIONAL PUBLIC RADIO FIRST 100 DAYS

"An important key to self-confidence is preparation."

- Arthur Ashe

My first 100 days at NPR were days of excitement and challenges. I was excited because I was leading one of the most reputable media organizations in the country. The challenges involved understanding how to manage this company with its unique culture. This provided a great learning curve for me. Now, I can take time and reflect on all that took place in my first four months.

In 1993, I had been with C&P Telephone Company for 20 years. Something was telling me that maybe my career had come to a plateau. In other words, it was not clear what my next position might be in the telephone company.

With my background and experience in law, public affairs and regulatory matters, I was uncertain if those skills would allow me to advance with the telephone company in the future. In other words, I was asking myself the tough question, "Where do I go from here?"

Toward the end of 1993, I received a phone call from the executive search firm of *Isaacson and Miller* of Boston, Massachusetts. The call came from Arnie Miller personally, who was a principal in the firm. He quickly got to the point and said, "Del, this is Arnie Miller from the firm Isaacson and Miller. The Board of National Public Radio has contracted us to find a President for NPR."

My immediate response was, "Why are you calling me?" Arnie replied, "I lived in Washington working in the White House under President Carter and I read about you and your career in government and business. I thought you might be interested in this opportunity so I'd like to take you to lunch to talk about it". I was deeply flattered and excited and I knew that such decisions required time and thought, along with discussing the opportunity with Gayle.

As I hung up the phone, I realized this might be the new leadership opportunity I had been seeking in light of my situation at C&P. Gayle thought it would be a great and fun challenge and so I researched the organization.

NPR is a non-profit organization that is supported by government subsidies and public outreach contributions. It has a long history of providing excellent programming and informative quality news. The more I looked into the company, the more it felt like a good fit.

First, I knew it was an opportunity to lead, and second, it was an opportunity for me to utilize my skills. I was not a journalist and I had never been involved with live programming, however, the opportunity to take my leadership skills and apply them to a not-profit news and information organization was a risk and challenge I would take on.

Later in the week, I called Arnie Miller back and agreed to have lunch. Arnie spent time discussing the job description for the Presidency of National Public Radio. He emphasized that the NPR Board was looking for a non-journalist with business experience in communications. I was quite pleased that my background might be a good fit.

Shortly thereafter, I discussed the NPR opportunity with Gayle and we both agreed it would be a fun challenge. I called Arnie and told him I would like to be considered for the job of President of National Public Radio. He seemed thrilled that I would "throw my hat in the ring." He said he would get back to me with more details shortly.

The vetting process moved fairly quickly and Arnie was keeping me in the loop. I later found out that there were some 200 other candidates in the running.

Arnie called and asked if would be available to interview before the Board of Directors of NPR. It would be a half-day of questions from the Board and my presentation of why I wanted the job.

We agreed upon a date and I prepared. Early on from my days as a young school boy and all throughout my days at Kansas University and in law school, a face-to-face interview was something I always did well. I had the skills to study the company inside and out and was gifted with a keen insight on what may be asked of me ahead of time. My educational upbringing taught me how to present myself in front of others and to always be willing to listen first and respond directly to what I was being asked. This was my comfort zone and I was ready.

Then, just one day before the interview, I got a call from Arnie. He said, "Del, we have now narrowed our search down from 200 to just 2. The interviews are scheduled for tomorrow and a decision will be made by the Board by tomorrow evening. My interview was in the morning and later that evening, I was offered the job as President of NPR.

In January 1994, I officially became President of National Public Radio. It was an exciting time and new page in my career. I was familiar with some of the more public challenges facing the 600 stations throughout the country, but I must admit, the structure of how the company operated was very new and somewhat foreign. I knew that I was on a learning curve.

The NPR business model was not my only challenge when I arrived on the scene. Federal Government funding became an issue. The Speaker of the House of Representatives, Newt Gingrich, was adamant about defunding all public broadcasting and had started a campaign to do so in late December 1993 before I arrived.

On December 6[th,] The Speaker was interviewed on a conservative cable channel and said, *"One of the things we're going to do this year, I hope, is to zero out the Corporation for Public Broadcasting, which has been eating taxpayers' money."*

He also said that the nearly $300 million the corporation gets in Federal money amounted to having the public pay 'involuntary' taxes.

This was a huge issue to face as I began my first 100 days. I knew I had my work cut out for me so I hit the ground running. This agenda by Gingrich not only affected NPR, but also The Public Broadcasting System (PBS, so I immediately contacted Ervin Duggan who was the President of PBS.

Ervin and I worked well together and became good friends on a mission. He knew of my political background and my ties to Capitol Hill. He asked me to take the lead and organize a game plan to defeat the Gingrich defunding proposal.

I contacted the NPR station managers from around the country and urged them to meet in Washington so we could organize and let our voices be heard. I also urged the stations to spread the word to their contributors and listeners informing them that NPR and PBS were under siege and the future of public broadcasting was in jeopardy. This was very important for the smaller stations within the network. Some of our medium-to-large stations didn't rely as much on the government subsidy, but for the smaller ones, it was vital to their existence.

With our work with Ervin Duggan and the PBS team, our lobbying plan on Capital Hill came together. After many meetings and hearings, we prevailed and the funding was kept intact. This was an exhilarating feeling and a great accomplishment in my early days on the job at NPR.

Soon after my arrival, I was faced with some internal issues at the main headquarters. There had been several discrimination lawsuits filed by minority employees. These employees felt as though they had been overlooked for promotions and their voices were not being heard. They believed it was discriminatory and based solely on race.

Now, as an African American and the newly elected president, I could feel the tension and pressure on me to act decisively on their behalf. I needed to put on my lawyer hat and think this through logically and thoroughly. I needed to do this right.

I determined that a defined process for advancement and promotions was critically needed. In fact, to my amazement, NPR did not have a Human Resources department to investigate and resolve these kinds of complaints. I quickly went on a search for a qualified person to lead this effort and be sensitive to the issues facing the company. I hired an African American woman, Kathleen Jackson, who did an outstanding job sorting through the issues and righting the ship. It was a much-needed piece to the company puzzle.

After about a month on the job and putting out fires non-stop, things seemed to quiet down and this gave me time to implement my vision for NPR moving forward. I knew I had the skills to make good changes that would advance the company in many directions. The question, however, was did I have the power and the support? The answer was, "not really."

I must admit that when I took the job, I did not completely understand the infrastructure of the company. The NPR Board was comprised of seventeen members: six at-large members, ten station managers, and the CEO. As you can see, the ten station managers had controlling power on the Board. The station managers were our customers and as board members they could hire and fire the CEO. This was a unique business model in which I was unaccustomed.

The Chairman of the Board at the time was Carl Matthusen. He was also the station manager of two radio stations in Phoenix, Arizona. Carl had a vested interest in my success as he was a part of the search committee that had recommended me for hire. I felt I needed to air out my frustrations about the infrastructure and the business model. I wanted to express to Carl that I may not be the man for this job.

I set up a meeting with Carl in Washington DC. Meanwhile, I gathered all of my thoughts, strategies and ideas and put them on paper. My goal was to convince Carl that the system needed to be changed in order for the organization to grow. I needed him as a partner to help me convince the board. After Carl arrived, we met for a private meeting in the NPR Board room.

The morning of our meeting, I set up easels with flip charts around the room to graphically display my points of view. I was ready for action. I spent a good hour going over my positions while he listened intently, often shaking his head in agreement, but saying little. At the end of my presentation, which consisted of my pointing out what was wrong with NPR, Carl quietly took the floor.

He basically said that this might not be the exact job I had envisioned, however, in life one must adapt. He explained that some of these station managers have been doing things a certain way for decades and change was difficult. However, he pointed out to me that if I could learn how the other side thinks and get more involved in the business of radio, that I would find it much easier later to make necessary changes.

This was a huge wakeup call for me. At that moment I knew I must make a choice – do I stay the course and get more involved in radio, or do I pack up my office and resign? I did what I knew I should do and stayed the course.

Over the next six months, I got more involved with the station managers and employees. I traveled the country supporting their efforts, all the while selling them on new programming we were developing in Washington. These stations were not only our customers, but they were our partners. Once I understood that, I knew I could manage, and manage I did.

What once seemed like a very unlikely fit for me turned out to be a perfect one. This was very humbling, but important to my business growth. I learned so much from these stations and at the same time I was beginning to slowly implement proper change. It was all working.

I spent almost five years as the President of National Public Radio. When I left, I felt I had done more than a good job. I believe I left NPR in much better shape than I had found it. Interestingly enough, my successor said just that. He thanked me for laying the groundwork for what was becoming a much more business-like infrastructure. I told him that by no means could I take the credit, and I meant it; Carl Matthusen is really the one that gave it to me straight and I thank him for that.

Today, no matter what part of the country I awake in, I find the station and listen to National Public Radio to start my day.

CABLEVISION FOR DC

> **"The future belongs to those who see possibilities before they become obvious."**
>
> *- John Scully*

When I went to work for Walter Fauntroy in 1971 as his Chief of Staff in the United States House of Representatives, my main job was to oversee a strong and forward-thinking staff that I could rely upon to help Walter achieve his agenda.

Harley Daniels was the legislative director, and Robert (Bob) Johnson was in charge of press and public relations. Geraldine Boykin was recruited to run the Congressional Liaison office in the city, referred to as the District Office. Shortly thereafter, I hired Howard Lee, a recent graduate of American University Law School, as a legal intern. These were the main players on the team. It was a good, strong group of talent and great minds.

I quickly learned that Bob Johnson had a talent for envisioning and organizing the public outreach for Walter Fauntroy. Therefore, all press directions and political campaign approaches were Bob's initiatives.

I found Bob to be very creative. He had good instincts about politics and was a good writer. Bob was central in helping Walter with both legislative and political strategy for the city.

Bob and I became good friends and colleagues because we both were interested in politics and the strategies behind politics. We made a good team on Walter's staff.

After a year and a half as Walter's Chief of Staff, I left to become the Public Affairs Manager for C&P Telephone Company in Washington DC. Bob left shortly thereafter and became an executive with the Cable Association.

Both Bob Johnson and I began new careers. I became an executive with the telephone company and Bob began his career in the cable business. During this time Bob and his wife, Sheila, founded Black Entertainment Television (B.E.T.), a cable network designed to appeal to an African American audience. It began with modest programing and eventually grew into a great powerhouse of news and entertainment.

Bob asked me to join his board at B.E.T., but I felt there were possible conflicts working in the telephone business so I didn't join the board in those early years.

While I was in my position at C&P Telephone Company, Bob called on me at my office to discuss a project he was pursuing outside of B.E.T. He was organizing a group to bid for the contract to build a new cable system for the District of Columbia. He continued and said, "I'd like to have you, along with the telephone company, as my partners on this bid."

This was surprising because telephone companies rarely talked to cable companies; they didn't have good relations. Also, from my position, I would need approval from the President of the company before entering into such a partnership. But the critical piece here was that it was a darn creative idea. Bob said, "You guys know everything about building underground and you also know how to build projects under budget and on time. Secondly, I want your political skills because that is what it's going to take, not only the technical abilities that you will bring from the telephone perspective, but your political abilities as assistant V.P. and things you've done in the community. I think with your help this will put my company in good standing to win this bid."

A long story short, I had to convince my superiors this was worth doing. So we agreed on a process where C&P Telephone Company was paid incrementally as each phase was completed. Having that settled, Bob and I went to work on the lobbying side.

Three groups were bidding for the opportunity to build the cable system for the city. Bob's group was District Cablevision Inc. The other two bidders were Capital City Cable and District Telecommunications Development Corp. The bid to build the system for the city was treated like legislation. The bid had to go through the Committee on Business and Economic Development. Once the bid was recommended out of committee, it had to pass the full council and then be signed by the mayor.

Unfortunately, our group was not the group recommended out of committee. Capital City Cable. a very strong group headed by, Wiley A.

Branton, former Dean of Howard University Law School along with Percy E. Sutton of New York, former Manhattan Borough President, was recommended by the Chair of the committee, Councilwoman Betty Ann. Kane. The full Council had the discretion to support the recommendation out of the committee or to name one of the other bidders.

So Bob and I went to work. We lobbied each member of the City Council personally. We stressed the merits of our group.

1. We offered the strong operational and technical experience that C&P Telephone Company. had in building systems on time and under budget.
2. Our group with more than 100 investors had a substantial number of minority investors with business and political connections.
3. There were two major cable companies as investors in our group - TCI and United Cable.

The full Council voted not only to disregard the recommendation for Capital City Cable but gave full approval to our group. We won the bid!

Just like other legislation, the selection by the City Council, of Bob Johnsons private group in partnership with the Telephone Company, had to be approved by the Mayor. The Mayor signed the bill and I can say with pride that the system was built under budget and on time.

I DIDN'T SEE THIS ONE COMING

> **"Let us now set forth one of the fundamental truths about marriage: the wife is in charge."**
>
> *- Anonymous*

Sometimes when we are too busy at work, we can lose focus on what matters outside of work. This is what happened to me as I was trying to become the best president of National Public Radio I could be.

I was really hitting my stride, getting familiar with how to manage a non-profit enterprise. I enjoyed going out into the field and visiting stations throughout the country. When I worked at C&P, I spent most hours and days navigating business within the walls of the headquarters. This was no longer the case.

In the spring of 1996 I visited the public radio station in Las Cruces, New Mexico, KRWG, at New Mexico State University (NMSU). I was invited by the development officer, Jeanna Carter, to speak to the community. I first met Jeanna when she was working with NPR Board Member Anthony Dean who served on the Board of National Public Radio when I was appointed to become president. I met her when visiting the NPR station at the University of Alabama in Tuscaloosa.

Upon arrival, I was given a warm welcome at KRWG. I met the Station Manager, Colin Gramansky and several other employees. I got a grand tour of the campus. I was enjoying this Southwest visit. This was my first time ever in New Mexico. It was beautiful.

Later that evening, a reception was held for me at the Bunch Gallery. This was a family-owned gallery in the heart of Mesilla, a small town adjacent to Las Cruces. Carolyn and Henry Bunch owned it. I toured the gallery and then addressed the gathering. I spoke a few words about the state of NPR and how it related to their station in New Mexico. I wanted to give them some insight on what we were doing in Washington to form a more cohesive relationship between the headquarters and the stations. The gathering was well attended. My remarks were well received.

After returning home to Potomac, Maryland, Gayle wanted to know about my visit to New Mexico. I told her I did not get the chance to see many parts of the area because the trip was short; however, what I saw I thought was beautiful.

She said that she had always wanted to go visit New Mexico again. Twice, as a teenager, she had been there with her parents and felt a kindred spirit with the Southwest. She told me she would love to go back and visit Las Cruces if I would be interested.

Well, this should have been my first sign, but being me and somewhat oblivious to nudges, I simply said sure, I would love to go. All along I was thinking it would be sometime near the end of the year or maybe early the following year before we would make the trip.

Well, that was not to be the case. Gayle quickly organized a trip for us in May of 1996 and I admit, I was excited to go back and explore. We planned to rent a car after we landed because flights to Las Cruces are served by the airport at El Paso, Texas. We would then have a 45-minute drive west to Las Cruces. This would be fun.

We located the Hilton Hotel where I had made a reservation. We were struck by the beauty of the Organ Mountains to the east of Las Cruces. We felt right then that Las Cruces, with these surroundings, might be the perfect place for a second home.

As we looked, we gravitated towards a dormant volcano named Picacho Peak. At the base of Picacho Peak was a new residential community. We drove through the community where we found beautiful homes, a golf course, swimming pools and so much charm. It had a lovely, warm feeling and was very welcoming.

As we were touring the area, we stopped to look at one of the open houses. We met the real estate agent who introduced herself as Maureen Pollock. She offered to help us as best she could.

We were happy to meet her and explained that we were new to New Mexico and were just here for a few days and trying to get a feel for the area. She was very helpful and not at all pushy. Before leaving, we exchanged numbers and she told us to contact her if we had questions while we were visiting.

Later that evening, once we got back to the hotel and were just settling in and dusk was upon us, we noticed a message light on our hotel phone. I picked up the phone to find it was a voice message from Maureen Pollack. She said on the message, "It was great meeting you guys today and I'm going to be cooking dinner for my boyfriend at his house this evening. We would love to have you join us. His name is Jim and he is a professor at NMSU. Would you give me a call after you get this message?"

I called back and told her that we'd love to join them. She gave us the address and the time and was quick to say she did not want to come across like a pushy realtor and this call was personal. This was quite a nice surprise and one we welcomed. We said to ourselves that Maureen's hospitality was a positive reflection on Las Cruces.

Once we arrived, she said again that she was not trying to sell us anything but just enjoyed our time together that afternoon and wanted to extend the invitation for dinner. Her boyfriend was a very interesting man and we enjoyed getting to know him.

After dinner, knowing we had only another day or two left, Maureen pulled out maps of the area and educated us on Las Cruces. The next day, Gayle and I looked at the areas recommended by Maureen and we kept coming back to the little town of Mesilla. A small restaurant with a bar anchored one end of the plaza in Mesilla and on the other end was a beautiful and historic Catholic church. Quaint little shops surrounded the entire area.

Each time driving through Mesilla, we kept our eye on several houses we liked. We called Maureen to help us out and explained to her we liked Mesilla and had our eye on a couple of homes. She explained that one house we liked she knew a lot about because she had built it. This was great news. It was a 3-bedroom house very near Mesilla that we knew we wanted to pursue. As time was approaching for us to return to DC, we actually did a good faith handshake with Maureen to buy this home. It was located at 1865 Mesilla Hills Road. This was to be our new second home.

It's now late 1996 going on 1997 and I am working hard at NPR. I had many challenges and I had never traveled this much. We had finalized the purchase of the house in New Mexico and were very happy with our new retreat outside of Washington DC. Gayle was elated as she now had a nice getaway that offered peace and beautiful views.

We were in New Mexico enjoying our wonderful new home at Christmas time 1996. We loved the weather with little rain or snow. While the evenings were cool, it was always sunny and pleasant in the daytime. This was a real treat for both of us.

I will never forget the conversation we had one evening. Gayle looked at me and announced that she planned to stay in Las Cruces during the months of January, February and March.

I was dumbfounded. I said, "Gayle, what do you mean you are going to spend three months here? We have a beautiful home in Maryland and I have a great job that I am committed to. I don't understand."

She said, "Delano, you can come visit, I'll be glad to travel with you and we can see the world, but I am not going to live in the DC area full time". Well, at this point, I was able to see the pieces of the puzzle coming together. I must admit, I was a slow learner in seeing Gayle's master plan, but eventually the light bulb lit up and I got it.

What Gayle was saying was that after 30+ years in Washington and raising a family and supporting all my efforts (although she wasn't complaining), she just felt it was time to leave. She knew there must be more to life than what we were living, and she was right.

The hardest part for me was coming to terms with leaving my job. I have never understood or been able to rationalize not working. It has always been a part of me and I felt that as a communicator and leader, I had to finish what I started.

Gayle didn't disagree, however, she quickly pointed out that I can lead and communicate from anywhere in the world and it need not be with NPR. It was time to take another huge leap of faith. I told her I would need time and it would take at least six months to phase down. I had to give notice to the NPR Board, begin sharing my decision with the senior team and to phase down with stations around the country. This process took longer than anticipated; it actually took more than a year before I felt comfortable letting go.

In early summer of 1998, I resigned from National Public Radio and Gayle and I made the move to New Mexico. It was an amazing time in both our lives. Gayle knew that it was important to take a stand at this time. She had a very strong sense of when it was time for change.

For me, it was very liberating. I had no job and nothing on the horizon. I was still active with two corporate boards, but no full time job. I didn't think I would feel so at ease, but I did, and it was a refreshing feeling to just let go.

We arrived in Las Cruces in mid-summer 1998 and settled into our home at 1865 Mesilla Hills Drive. Now that I look back I can say, "I surely didn't see this one coming!"

PHONE CALL THAT CHANGED MY LIFE

> "A good head and a good heart are always a formidable combination."
>
> - *Nelson Mandela*

In the fall of 1998 we made the decision that the house we were living in at 1865 Mesilla Hills Drive in New Mexico was too small. We had six grandkids now and enjoyed having everyone under one roof when they came to visit. This just wasn't comfortably possible with our present home.

Later in the year, around November, a house just up the road in the same neighborhood was up for sale. Gayle wanted to look to see if this house would be one we would like. At first glance, I didn't like the structure of the house. It just seemed too boxy. Gayle, however, convinced me there wouldn't be any harm in looking.

We contacted a realtor and set up an appointment to view the inside, but unfortunately on that day, the realtor had to cancel. However, the owners of the home were more than willing to let us look. The house was at 7140 Las Vistas Drive and it was about a 5-minute walk from our present home. We loved the neighborhood and had made good friends, so finding something in the same area was a huge priority for us.

As we drove up the big hill towards the house, I was still very skeptical on several fronts. Not only did I not like the architecture, it was listed as just having two bedrooms. I kept thinking to myself this place may have more land, but it won't meet our needs with only two bedrooms. I kept quiet for the short ride to the house and tried to be optimistic.

As we entered the home, we were immediately met with the beautiful view of the Organ Mountains seen from the dining area. The owners continued to show us around and as we approached the kitchen, we could see a deck on the outside. From there we could see an amazing panoramic view of more than I could have ever imagined. The Organ Mountains and the Dona Ana range and the Robledo Mountains were visible from so many directions. We could also see the Franklin Mountains near El Paso, Texas. It was incredible.

We then looked at the master bedroom which was quite large and very nice. At this point my thoughts were conflicted; I liked the views but still wasn't convinced this was the house for us. I kept telling myself to just be quiet and enjoy the tour.

Then we followed the owners downstairs to the second bedroom. It was below the main dining area and was nicely laid out. It was spacious with its own bath and shower and there was a large family area.

Throughout the tour, I would glance at Gayle and could see her mind turning with ideas. I am convinced Gayle was an architect in a former life. She had incredible vision with what could be done on a piece of property. Again, keeping quiet and enjoying the tour, I waited until we were headed back home to share my thoughts.

Once we got back home, Gayle shared her vision. She went on about how we could expand with the unused land and make this a true dream house. I was intrigued by her thoughts. The view was spectacular and was almost enough to seal the deal for me, but Gayle's thoughts put it all into perspective. We agreed to make an offer.

Sure enough, our offer was accepted and soon we became the proud owners of 7140 Las Vista Drive, just up the hill from our present home. Then we put our first home on the market and became excited about all the possibilities with the new home. However, we were much less excited about the packing and boxing that was ahead. Here we go again.

Two weeks later we were immersed in packing and trying our best to enjoy this time-consuming task. Our goal was to get most of the stuff boxed up in the mornings so we could enjoy the evenings with a bottle of wine and relax.

One day while boxing stuff up and labeling each box with what was inside, we both heard the phone ring. Looking at each other and wondering where the phone might be hiding, Gayle finds it and picks it up. I can hear her answer and then I hear her say, "Yes, he is here."

She looks across the room at me and whispers as she hands the phone to me. "It's the Vice President of the United States calling!"

Now I am sure if I could see a picture of my face at that moment it would show disbelief. I quickly gathered my composure and took the phone. I said, "Mr. Vice President, to what do I owe this honor?"

He says, "Del, this is Al." Then his voice turned very official and he continued. "Del, I am calling on behalf of President Clinton and the President would like to nominate you as the next Ambassador to the Republic of South Africa."

I said, "What did you say Mr. Vice President?" (I didn't intend for him to repeat himself but he did.)

Then, I whispered to Gayle, "The President wants to nominate me as the next United States Ambassador to South Africa."

She whispers back, "Yes, yes, yes!" as she is nodding her head up and down.

I quickly get back on the phone and say, "Mr. Vice President, I accept."

He says, "Congratulations, you will be hearing from The State Department." *CLICK*

This was the beginning of a life changing moment. Once again while moving, from one house to another, very much the way it happened in 1966 before departing for the Peace Corps in Nigeria, our lives were changed in an instant.

Gayle and I continued to gush with excitement and for the most part were now useless as far as packing goes. We enjoyed the moment and the evening replaying that call again and again through our heads. It was a restless night of sleep for sure, so many plans and so much to look forward to.

The next couple of days were just as busy. We received a call from the State Department and the process began in full force. Days later we received many documents from the State Department that we needed to fill out and send back. They contained every question imaginable. It was a tedious process, but one well worth it.

It's now getting close to Christmas of 1998 and we were told by the State Department that until I was officially nominated, no one could know about it. This was becoming hard for Gayle and me. We wanted to share the news and excitement with our kids. One day, we called the State Department and asked if we could share the news. They told us yes, as long as it was with the immediate family, it would be okay.

We were excited. This was great news! We waited until after Christmas to plan a conference call with everyone on the phone. We wanted to let them know we had good news to share. We wanted this to be another *Forced Family Fun* event.

The day came and everyone called in. The families were all eager to hear the news, but not nearly as excited as we were to share. I remember telling everyone the story about how it all came about, the call from the Vice President and so on. There was absolute silence on the phone; I could tell that everyone was in awe.

And then as I knew I would, I broke into tears of joy. Everyone congratulated us and we reminded them all to keep this very hush. The conversation then quickly turned to answering questions like, "When can we come visit?" and

"How far is the plane ride?" It was a wonderful celebration in the New Year.

As time went on, I wondered just how my name surfaced to the top of the nominations list. I had never put my name in a hat nor had I been contacted about any possible appointments. So curiosity got the best of me and I just needed to know.

In early February I made a call to Bob Nash. Bob was the Head of Presidential Personnel. I knew him well and I called him because I knew he could tell me exactly how this all came about.

I got Bob on the phone and he was more than willing to share the process. He told me that my name was high on the list for appointments for ambassadorships to African countries and my name was at the top of the list for South Africa.

Bob said that he was in the Oval Office with President Clinton, Vice President Al Gore, Secretary of State Madeleine Albright, and Sandy Berger who was National Security Advisor to the President. Bob said the topic was about ambassadorial nominations and when they got to South Africa, my name was on the top of the list.

That's when the President spoke up and said, "Al, I understand that Delano is retired somewhere in New Mexico and one of us should call him to let him know how important this assignment is."

Al said, "I'll call him, Mr. President."

So that's how it all came about. I knew I could get the "inside info" from Bob Nash and that's exactly how it all played out. Vice President Gore called and it changed my life forever.

ONE DAY AT A TIME

> **"The best thing about the future is that it comes one day at a time."**
>
> *- Abraham Lincoln*

As 1999 unfolded, the Ambassadorial nomination and confirmation process impacted my life. It's an incredible honor to be nominated as the next United States Ambassador to the Republic of South Africa.

It is also an arduous process to become confirmed. It was important for me to learn as much as I could about South Africa, its people, its cultures, and its challenges.

It was important for me to learn about post-apartheid South Africa, its newly formed parliamentary government facing the challenging issues of education, housing, health and jobs. An important part of being the United States Ambassador to South Africa is to understand our foreign policy and its impact on South Africa and the continent.

The confirmation process was challenging. In March 1999 I had still not received the formal nomination from the White House. I asked myself, why haven't I received the nomination? The call from Vice President Gore came in November last year." It was my assumption that I was not competing against anyone for the position, since I had received the call directly from the White House. Why is it taking so long?

After many calls back and forth with the South Africa Desk at the State Department, it appeared that the White House was nervous about making premature announcements on nominations. In other words, the White House wanted to wait until all of my background checks had been completed before the formal nomination was announced.

The State Department explained that the White House had previously been embarrassed by announcing nominations publically before the background checks had been completed; then having to withdraw the nomination because of issues in the background check.

I waited and waited and finally in June 1999, I received the formal nomination from the White

House. It was official; I was nominated by President Clinton for the United States Ambassadorship to the Republic of South Africa.

The next part of the process was going through a confirmation hearing by the Sub-Committee on Africa of the Senate Foreign Relations Committee. To be a United States Ambassador, you must be nominated by the President with the advice and consent of the United States Senate. In some cases, the nomination becomes a partisan, political issue and the nomination can be held up without a hearing.

In my case, I was nominated by President Clinton, a Democrat. Some Republicans were delaying his nominations for political and sometimes ideological reasons. This could mean that my nomination, as well as other nominations for Presidential appointments, could be held up by this political back and forth between Senators. I was never sure of the reasons why.

Several weeks after my nomination in June 1999, President Clinton nominated former Senator Carol Moseley Braun of Illinois for the Ambassadorship to New Zealand. Jesse Helms, a Republican senator from North Carolina announced his staunch opposition to her nomination. In fact, Helms said, "She will be confirmed over my dead body." I became very nervous that this might further delay my nomination as well.

With this back and forth political wrangling over nominations, I felt as if I may never get confirmed by the Senate. Since, Carol Moseley Braun had been a part of this prestigious club, the United States Senate, I doubted that her nomination would be defeated.

The process in the United States Senate allows for voice votes on less controversial matters. If the issue is contested or becomes controversial, the procedure requires debates and roll call votes. To my surprise, Braun's nomination did pass the Senate Foreign Relations Committee and was brought to the Senate floor for debate and vote. She was approved 96-2. After she was finally confirmed, I felt this was good news and there would be hope for me.

Finally, I received word that the nine nominees for different posts in Sub-Saharan Africa would have their hearings in early August 1999. The State Department received a call from the

Senate sub-committee on Africa of the Foreign Relations committee, saying they would like to divide the nine ambassadorial nominees' hearings into two panels: five nominees on the first, and then four nominees on the second.

Then the committee advised that the nominee for the United States Ambassador to the Republic of South Africa should be assigned to the smaller second panel, to be scheduled later in the afternoon because they had more questions for him. This certainly added pressure to my preparations for the hearing. I was being singled out for more questions by the panel and my fellow nominees appeared to feel less pressure. In fact, they kidded me about my receiving such attention.

The hearings proceeded before the subcommittee on Africa, chaired by Senator Russ Feingold, Democrat of Wisconsin. The ranking Republican was Senator Bill Frist from Tennessee. They presided over the hearings for the nine nominees.

My son, Geoffrey, and his wife, Lisa, and my two grandsons, Geoffrey Jr and Justin, attended the confirmation hearing with my wife, Gayle. I was a little reluctant to have too many family members there because I didn't know how difficult the process would be and how well I would respond.

I studied, read and talked with people about South Africa, Sub-Saharan Africa, and specifically the countries around South Africa. I wanted to have a sense of our Foreign Policy, our challenges and a sense of the direction of our State Department toward South Africa and other countries. Yes, it was true. The subcommittee did have more questions for me.

Before my panel was called, my grandson, Justin, who was almost 10 years old, was talking to a TV cameraman there to cover the hearing. I overheard the conversation and Justin introduced himself and asked the cameraman who he was. He said, "I'm with the South African Broadcasting Company and your grandfather is going to be on television in South Africa later tonight."

I was excited and a little nervous. I got through the panel in good shape. Although the questions were not that tough, I had been well prepared by the State Department. I had done a lot of work and study, and my hearing was very successful.

After several days, I received word from the State Department that five of the nine nominees had been approved, but four of the nine had not been approved. I was one of the four. I was very disappointed and very concerned. Why didn't I get approved?

After many inquiries by the State Department to the Senate Committee, we discovered that the five nominees who had been approved had school age children. It was August and they needed to get to their posts in order to get their children into school. The four of us who did not get approved at this time did not have school age children. I was relieved.

The Senate was out for recess in August 1999, so I returned to New Mexico. At least I would be waiting for the decision on confirmation in a cooler climate and away from the heat in Washington DC.

I continued to read, study, and talk to people about the issues and challenges of the embassy and the State Department in Sub-Saharan Africa. I was hopeful that when the Senate returned in September, I would get my confirmation.

During the wait for confirmation, we were required to attend a 2-week course to teach us how to handle the day-to-day tasks of running an embassy.

There were 13 Diplomats in my class. We had been assigned to different posts around the world. Spouses were invited into the sessions that were not classified. When the Ambassadorial candidates attended classified sessions, a special session was held for spouses. We learned all about the administrative side of the embassy. We learned about press relations and public relations. We role-played on specific issues that might confront us as diplomats. It was an exciting course.

In the U.S. Foreign Service, there are career ambassadors and non-career ambassadors (political appointees). I was a political appointee of President Clinton. A career ambassador and a non-career ambassador chaired the 2-week course. I learned so much from my colleagues. As ambassadorial designees, since we had not yet been confirmed, we were scheduled to meet with Secretary of State Madeleine Albright.

In preparation for the meeting with Secretary Albright, we were lined up alphabetically outside her office. The 13 of us were lined up and I was in the middle. As we had rehearsed it, our names would be called and we were to step forward and shake the hand of the Secretary of State. After every person had been introduced along with his or her spouse, we went into the Secretary's office for a brief meeting.

Gayle and I had known Secretary Albright over the years in Washington DC. I remember when she worked for Senator Ed Muskie and was very active in politics and community activities in Northwest Washington. We had worked together and had respect for each other.

As I was standing in line, I was asking myself, what is the proper protocol in my meeting Madeleine Albright now that she is the Secretary of State? Since I new the Secretary, was it proper protocol to give her a hug or should I just shake her hand?

Then my name was called, "Ambassadorial Designee Delano Lewis and Mrs. Gayle Lewis.".

I stepped forward and as I was putting my hand out, she said, "Del!" and gave me a big hug. So much for proper protocol! My colleagues ribbed me about my favored treatment by the Secretary of State.

SWORN IN AS AMBASSADOR

> **"He that can have patience can have what he will."**
>
> - *Benjamin Franklin*

I received a telephone call from the desk officer of the State Department in early November 1999 and the caller said, "Mr. Lewis?"

I said, "Yes."

"Or should I say, Mr. Ambassador?"

I said, "Oh, have I been confirmed?"

She said, "Yes, we just got word that you and the three of your colleagues have been confirmed as ambassadors."

I said, "Oh, hooray! Hooray!" I was very excited. Gayle was not there when I received the phone call; she had gone out to an event with a neighbor. I ran around the house all excited and I decided to put up congratulatory banners and signs. My plan was to turn the lights low so when

162

Gayle came in I would surprise her with the announcement that I finally received confirmation for the ambassadorship! Champagne was chilled and ready.

It was getting dark and Gayle had still not returned. When I heard the neighbor's car pull into the driveway, I turned the lights down low. I waited for Gayle to come in. She and our neighbor were just sitting in the car continuing their conversation.

Gayle finally came in the house and I shouted:

"SURPRISE! I have been confirmed!"

I turned up the lights and we had a big hug. We opened the champagne and we toasted my confirmation. It was an exciting time in our lives and this appointment was the pinnacle of my career.

I was so honored to be selected to serve in South Africa. This country was at the dawn and the awakening of a new democracy. The "apartheid regime" had been dismantled and the majority Black population was free from the dominating minority white government. Freedom fighters like Nelson Mandela, Walter Sisulu, Helen

Suzman and many others had prevailed. With democratic elections held in 1994, Nelson Mandela became President after being released from prison where he had served over twenty-seven years.

It was a thrill for me to serve in South Africa, a country on a path to building a strong democracy. Nelson Mandela served only one five-year term then chose not to run again in 1999. He was succeeded by his Deputy President, Thabo Mbeki who was elected President in 1999.

It is required before you are confirmed, to have the approval of your nomination as ambassador by the president of the receiving country. Since President Mandela chose not to run in 1999 and Thabo Mbeki was elected his successor, the United States government asked for the approval of my nomination from both leaders.

I received the approval of both Mandela and Mbeki and began planning for my Swearing In at the State Department. We chose to have a small ceremony at the State Department for family and friends. I asked Chief Judge, John Conway, of the Federal District Court in New Mexico, to swear me in. We had been classmates at the Washburn School of Law in Topeka, Kansas.

John and I graduated together in June 1963. John went to New Mexico to practice law. Later he was elected to the State Senate. John had a successful law practice before being appointed a Federal Judge.

When I called John and asked if he would swear me in, he responded, "Well, I would be honored, but I've got to check the regulations." This was typical John.

I said, "John, you know as a sitting judge you have every authority to swear me in as a U.S. Ambassador."

It was a beautiful day. We had our family there, our grandchildren and friends. The Assistant Secretary for Africa, Susan Rice, was there and she gave introductory remarks on behalf of the State Department.

The South African Ambassador to the United States, Sheila Sisulu, who was also the daughter-in-law of freedom fighter Walter Sisulu, was there and she spoke at the ceremony. When John swore me in as Gayle held the Bible, both he and I were crying. It was a momentous occasion.

As I was going to the podium to give my remarks, I turned back and thanked John for doing the honor of swearing me in and then I said to him, "John, we aren't in Kansas anymore," a line from the *Wizard of Oz,* a small tribute to our Kansas roots.

Gayle and I had a scheduled visit with President Clinton and a picture taken with him in the Oval Office.

I had received the call from Vice President Gore about the nomination in November 1998. It is now December 1999; over a year from the time I got the call. We wanted to get to South Africa as soon as we could because as a political appointee, I would have to resign if there was a change of parties in the upcoming American election.

So we prepared to go to our post according to our orders, which included a visit to the American military command base at Stuttgart, Germany. This was the U.S. military support base for all American Embassies in Sub Saharan Africa. They wanted me to meet the Commander and others to get an understanding of the U.S. military support for our post in South Africa.

We spent a couple of days in Stuttgart and then we headed on to South Africa. We landed in Johannesburg where we were met by Embassy staff who drove us to the Ambassadorial residence. Like the American Embassy, the Ambassadorial residence is located in Pretoria which is about thirty miles from the airport.

We landed on December 22, 1999; over a year from the time I got the call from the White House. This was just the beginning of a very exciting time.

CREDENTIALS CEREMONY IN SOUTH AFRICA

> **"Success comes when people act together; failure tends to happen alone.**
>
> *- Deepak Chopra*

After my confirmation, I was given a packet of material called *My Credentials*. It was a beautifully written set of principles that outlined my background and outlined my function as the President's official representative. It said that I would take orders through the Secretary of State from the President of the United States. I would be the President's personal representative to South Africa. Once I was there, it was protocol for me to present my credentials to the president of that country.

For many years now, I've been approached by students, friends, family and even strangers asking me what it was like being the Ambassador to South Africa. Most people want to know what I did while I was there and just what was my role.

To answer these questions, one must understand the role of an American Ambassador. An American Ambassador is the official representative of the President of The United States to the country to which he or she has been designated. In the U.S. Foreign Service, two-thirds of the Ambassadors are Foreign Service Officers who have earned the rank and position of ambassador. One-third of the Ambassadors are political appointees. Both the career and the political must be nominated by the President and confirmed by the United States Senate.

We arrived on December 22, 1999. It was summertime in South Africa and it was also vacation time. We discovered early that no business was being done because most people were on vacation or holiday from mid December through mid January. This was something to get used to. We not only had to get used to a new culture and a sense of what my new job was to be, but we were caught in vacation season as well.

However, even after the long confirmation process, the packing, the schooling and all the paperwork that took place before finally arriving, I was always aware that it was 1999 and the U.S. elections would be taking place in 2000. If the

Democratic Party did not get elected, I, as a political appointee, would have to come home.

We knew it was very possible we would have only a year in South Africa because there could be a political change of administration from Democrat to Republican after the elections in November 2000. We knew we had to work hard on our goals and do our best under the cloud of having to resign our post should that be the case.

Vice President Al Gore campaigned on the Democratic ticket against George W. Bush on the Republican ticket for President. After many election irregularities around the country, the election outcome was an issue before the U.S. Supreme Court. The Supreme Court ruled in favor of George W. Bush and he became the 43rd President of the United States. I served an additional six months after discussions with the new administration.

Now let me get back to the topic of this memory - CREDENTIALS CEREMONY IN SOUTH AFRICA - and share with you one of the most amazing times of my life. I had no idea the power, pomp and circumstance that would be involved with the credentials ceremony.

I was scheduled to present my credentials to President Mbeki in early February of 2000. There were several new ambassadors from other countries to South Africa and they would also present their credentials to President Mbeki. These were individual ceremonies; we did not present together.

The South African Office of Protocol wanted us to rehearse so we would be familiar with the protocol around the presentation of credentials. The ambassadors from Kuwait and from Egypt were also presenting their credentials on the same day, however not at the same time. I got to know them well because we started our careers in South Africa about the same time.

We had a choice of being picked up by the South African Government limousine either at the residence or at the Embassy. I decided that we wanted to be picked up from the Embassy. I discovered later this was highly unusual and very gratifying to the employees of the embassy. Previous American ambassadors when presenting their credentials had been picked up from the residence and the embassy didn't get to be a part of this very special occasion, so in this case, it was exciting for everyone.

On the day I presented my credentials, we gathered at the Embassy. The Embassy employees were all excited about this event. The United States Marine Guard was outside. We were waiting on the South African Government limousine to approach at the scheduled time. When it arrived, our Marine Guards saluted. The Chief of Protocol was in the lead car. He stepped out and told us we should go in the second car. Gayle and I had designated places where we had to sit in the limousine.

We went from our Embassy, which was about a five to ten-minute drive, to the South African Union building, where we would be presented to President Mbeki. When we stepped out of the limousine the military band played both national anthems. We entered into the hall and we were met by more South African government personnel, as well as press and news people snapping pictures. Gayle and I walked down a beautiful red carpet to the end of the hall to meet President Mbeki.

It would be an understatement to say that my knees were wobbling as I was approaching the President. I gave my short statement and I presented my credentials. As rehearsed, President

Mbeki said kind remarks and accepted my credentials. Mrs. Mbeki did not attend. I believe she was traveling. She did send her welcome and regards. Chief of Staff, Frank Chicane, was there and after the presentation and remarks, we went into the adjourning room where we had tea.

This was very cordial. We engaged in general chitchat getting to know one another. We talked about my background, we talked about the President Mbeki's agenda, and after about ten or fifteen minutes, we took our leave.

I have had many wonderful moments in my life that I cherish. This was one of the most incredible. The sophistication, along with the formality and the chilling awareness of what I was taking on, hit me with great emotion. I was a proud African American representing my country and did not believe it was all taking place.

There was a moment, if not two or three, where I just wished my mother could see me and watch me present my credentials. If not for anything else, to let her know that she was correct all along – I could do anything I put my mind to.

I also wished that my sons and their families could have been there. I know they have heard the stories and seen all the pictures, but to be in that moment, would have been so special.

Even as I write this memory in this very moment, it all comes back so vividly - the climate, the people, the pomp and circumstance, the glory, and the pride. I am blessed!

PAT GORVALLA

Before departing for South Africa, we had
been talking with our good friends from my Peace
Corps days, Olive and Hank Raullerson. They told
us that once we arrived in South Africa we should
meet their good friend, Pat Gorvalla. They
described her as a very prominent South African
businesswoman, whom we should meet and get to
know.

In early 2000, while we were resident in Cape
Town for the Parliamentary session of the South
African Government, we received a beautiful
invitation from Pat Gorvalla to attend her 70th
birthday party in Stellenbosch. We immediately
accepted and made plans to attend this formal gala
event. Our embassy staff advised me that this was
a very important invitation from an equally
important South African woman. One person at
the embassy said that we would be in for a treat –
and indeed we were.

Pat was a "colored" South African woman with a mixed ancestry. She had been married to a very prominent and successful "colored" South African businessman. He was deceased by the time we were in South Africa, but they had been in business together. They owned several small businesses including service stations and grocery stores. They had become very successful entrepreneurs.

It seemed to me that Pat had received every honor imaginable. We learned she was very active in the Anglican Church and had received an award from the church and had been honored by the South African government. She had been a freedom fighter and was highly respected around the country.

On the evening of her birthday party as we stood in the receiving line to greet Mrs. Govalla, we noticed that everyone in this line of 700 guests seemed to know Mrs. Gorvalla very well. When we reached the head of the line, she greeted us so warmly - she knew who we were!

She said, "Ambassador and Mrs. Lewis!" We realized later that we were the only invited guests she had never met. We became instant friends and that friendship blossomed over our year and a half in South Africa.

This was a sit-down dinner for some 700 people and the hall it was held in was beautiful. There was an orchestra and a choir from the Anglican Church. The assortment of foods and beverages was amazing and it indeed was a wonderful 70th birthday celebration for Pat.

She had arranged for us to be at a center table where we would be well taken care of. There were several people at that table who embraced us during our time in South Africa and we became close friends thereafter.

One person was James Dickinson Barker, who was a Trustee and Advisor to the Boschendal Winery. Another was an Episcopal bishop, George Swartz and his wife, Sylvia. He and his wife became very good friends of ours as well. It was a beautiful night and the beginning of a beautiful friendship in meeting Pat Gorvalla and others.

During our time in South Africa, we would socialize with Pat often. When she learned that my birthday was coming up in November 2000, she said, "I'd like to give you a birthday party at my house, why don't you put down maybe five couples you would like to have invited. I will also make some invites and I will have a special guest for you, and we will do it on the night of November 12th, your birthday."

I invited several people, including Paul and Roberta Kolp, my friends from our Peace Corps days. Paul had been with USAID in Benin City, Nigeria, when I was the Peace Corps Associate Director there. They were visiting us in South Africa so they were on my guest list.

I would have never guessed the surprise special guest. Soon after we all gathered in her parlor for drinks and hors d'oeuvres, Pat Gorvalla announced the special guest had arrived. I was shocked and honored. The special guest was Archbishop Desmond Tutu with his charming wife, Leah.

Desmond Tutu, an Archbishop in the Anglican Church, was an active pastor. He was very active in the anti-apartheid movement. Archbishop Tutu was a Freedom Fighter along with Nelson Mandela and others; and the

Archbishop won the Nobel Peace Prize for his efforts against apartheid.

This birthday party in the lovely home of Pat Gorvalla and having Archbishop Desmond Tutu come as the special guest for my party is a memory I will always cherish.

THE UNITED STATES MISSION TO SOUTH AFRICA

> **"Coming together is a beginning; keeping together is progress; working together is success."**
>
> *- Henry Ford*

I was impressed with our visit to Stuttgart, Germany, in December of 1999 as we were on our way to South Africa. We visited the United States European Command, which provided military support for all American Embassies in Sub-Saharan Africa.

I was also impressed with the Deputy Commander-in-Chief of the United States European Command, Admiral Charles S. Abbot. He was known as Admiral Steve Abbot. We stayed with the Admiral and Mrs. Abbot at their home. We were hosted and briefed by the Admiral and the Military Command staff.

Later, we were introduced to Ambassador Peter Chaveas, assistant to the Commander, and his wife, Lucille Chaveas. Ambassador Chaveas had been a Peace Corps volunteer in Chad and served as Ambassador to Malawi.

Lucille Chaveas gave Gayle a very helpful tip. She told her that as spouse of an American ambassador serving overseas she would have a great deal of power, the greatest of those powers being the power to convene. We both remembered this and Gayle used this tip with great success during our tour.

One of the most valuable lessons learned in the two-week training program for Ambassadors in Washington DC was the following:

As Ambassadors, you should develop a mission for your service in the country.

I took that advice to heart and Gayle and I discussed what would be our mission in South Africa. Early on, we had decided to lead as a partnership. I had read many reports and talked to many people about the challenges facing South Africa and how the embassy could be helpful.

Gayle and I developed a mission, and from the day we landed and from our first meeting with the senior echelon of the embassy in Pretoria, we clarified two points.

181

One point was that Gayle Lewis would be an integral part of the ambassadorship, short of being exposed to classified material. She would be involved with the projects we embarked upon during my time as ambassador. This was well received. Shortly after I made my introductory speech where I said this was a partnership between me, as the ambassador, and my spouse, the security officer said that he understood and that she would be invited to our first non-classified briefing at the Embassy after my speech.

The second point in my introductory remarks was the mission to South Africa. As we had read and thought about it, we wanted to focus on three areas of responsibility.

Our first area of focus would be in health. HIV and AIDS had spread throughout the country. It was becoming an epidemic. With the help of USAID (United States Agency for International Development) and the embassy staff, we could develop a program to help South Africans prevent the spread of the disease HIV/AIDS.

The second area was economic development. I wanted to bring my business experience to the embassy. My experience working with entrepreneurs and business leaders in the United States could be useful. I wanted to bring an understanding of how important foreign investment would be to a developing country like South Africa. I wanted economic development to be a cornerstone of our mission.

The third area was education. We firmly believed that whatever assistance the U.S. Embassy could give to the Ministry of Education would go a long way to uplifting the quality of life of the country. We firmly believed that education and skills training could uplift communities and increase prospects for the country.

U.S. AID TO MOZAMBIQUE

> **"It always seems impossible
> until it's done."**
> *- Nelson Mandela*

One aspect of an American Ambassador's job involves humanitarian aid and assistance. My experience called on all my diplomatic skills in trying to assist the flood victims in the country of Mozambique. In February and March of 2000, heavy rains caused extreme flooding in Mozambique

Mozambique is a country north of South Africa and on the Indian Ocean. It is economically poor while rich in culture. It is a coastal country with great seafood but not a lot of other natural resources. The government was stable but its economy was struggling.

In February and March 2000, continuous heavy rains along the coast caused flooding of disastrous proportions. We wanted to offer help from the American Embassy in South Africa. We had to work through the Foreign Ministry of South

Africa in order to offer our assistance to the people of Mozambique.

The Foreign Minister at this time was Madame Nkosazana Dlamini-Zuma. She was an ex-wife of the then Deputy President of South Africa, Jacob Zuma. She was a medical doctor and active in the anti-apartheid movement. She was also a strong ANC political person and close to President Mbeki.

The United Kingdom and other countries were also interested in giving aid to Mozambique. We discussed with the Foreign Minister and her staff the various ways this could happen.

It was our plan to gather the aid; blankets, food, tents and other supplies from the American military base in Stuttgart Germany. The supplies would be flown to South Africa and then airlifted to Mozambique. There was no landing strip sturdy enough to handle the cargo planes that would bring the supplies. This called for a diplomatic plan between these countries - the United States, South Africa and Mozambique.

The Foreign Minister called me to her office and said, "We have an issue here." She said,

"South Africa is a sovereign country and so is Mozambique. There will be no foreign governments using our country as a dispatching place for goods to another sovereign country without their permission." We had to get approval from the government of Mozambique before landing the goods in South Africa and having them organized to be airlifted to Mozambique. It could not appear that South Africa was doing any military intervention or any intervention in a sovereign country.

So this was one of the first diplomatic issues I had to resolve. I talked with the British High Commissioner, Dame Maeve Fort, a highly experienced diplomat (ambassadors from British Commonwealth countries to other British Commonwealth countries are titled, "High Commissioner"). I chatted with her and told her that if the U.K. was thinking about delivering goods through South Africa to Mozambique, the approval from Mozambique would be needed for this to happen.

She didn't believe me and said, "We are going to go ahead and do it anyway. I'm not sure all that is necessary; this is humanitarian aid."

I said, "Well, this is the order that I have from the South African Foreign Ministry and I'm going to make sure that we get this approval."

I worked with my Deputy Chief of Mission and as luck would have it, he was having lunch with some Mozambique officials and others. He got us a contact with the government of Mozambique and we presented our case that we needed approval from the government of Mozambique for us to land in South Africa before airlifting the supplies to Mozambique.

The required letter from the government of Mozambique was sent to the Foreign Ministry of South Africa but we still didn't have the final approval from South Africa.

Meanwhile, the U.S. General in Germany was very impatient with me. He said that the goods were already packed and they had a timetable for delivery.

He asked, "What is the matter with the U.S. government and the Ambassador's office? Why can't we get approval to land and what's going on?"

I understood his impatience. I told him that we were working hard but we had to go through diplomatic channels to make this happen. I was getting it from both sides. From one side I needed approval from the South African Foreign Minister. On the other side the American military General was ready to dispatch.

Given the situation, I realized that I needed to find a way to urge the Foreign Minister into action. It occurred to me that the President's office could be helpful. I had developed a good relationship with a counselor to the president so I called her that night and explained to her the issue at hand. The American military was ready to take off to bring humanitarian goods to Mozambique by dispatching them from South Africa. I told her that I had approval from Mozambique for this but I didn't have the final approval from Madame Zuma. I asked her if she could help. She said yes and that she would work on it.

After some tense moments, during the night, I received a call from the Counselor to the President telling me that the Foreign Minister had given her approval for us to proceed.

I quickly called the general at Stuttgart and said, "The mission is a go. We have approval to land in South Africa to deliver the goods to Mozambique."

As an aside, I heard later that the British High Commissioner did authorize flights from the U.K. to South Africa before getting approval from the South African government. Those planes were turned around mid-flight because they were not authorized to land in South Africa.

BOEING WINS CONTRACT IN SOUTH AFRICA

This memory is about economic development in South Africa.

In 2000, South Africa had a very good transportation system. The major roads were good, there was a good railroad system, and the major airports were modern and becoming more state of the art every year. South African Airways was a major player in international travel and South African Airways, and many smaller airlines, provided frequent and safe travel between the major cities of South Africa and the rest of the world.

In the year 2000, South African Airways was booming, led by an American CEO (Chief Executive Officer) named Coleman Andrews. It was a state-owned enterprise and growing steadily. South African Airways put out a bid to purchase sixteen new planes. Boeing Aircraft, a United States company entered the bidding ring, as did Airbus. The bid was for $2.3 billion dollars to build sixteen new planes for commercial passenger travel.

I was very excited about this possibility. Boeing had several executives on the ground in South Africa and they were working hard to win this bid. In the embassy, we had several officers who were active in business issues. The Economic Officer at the embassy was directly responsible for promoting American investment in South Africa.

I worked very closely with the Economic Officer, Bob Godec, to help Boeing Aircraft win the bid. Over time, I had made many speeches through the American Chamber of Commerce in South Africa on the importance of foreign investment in South Africa.

In many of my business speeches, I talked about promotion of American business and American investment in South Africa. It was one of my three goals and it was high on my mission. We had an opportunity to win this $2.3 billion dollar bid. Our major competitor was Airbus.

After several months, it became clear that Boeing was losing ground and their marketing strategy was not working. After discussions with Bob Godec, we decided to become more actively involved with the bid. It was decided that a different marketing strategy on the ground was needed if we were going to win against Airbus.

So I decided with the Economic Officer to reach out to the Chairman and CEO of Boeing, Phil Condit, to discuss our ideas on how best to win this bid.

Our plan was for a phone call to be set up between the Chairman/CEO and me at some designated time. During this period, the U.S. Secretary of Energy, Bruce Babbitt, was visiting South Africa. He was there for a conference on energy and the environment. At the conclusion of the conference, the embassy hosted a dinner in honor of the Secretary at a restaurant at the top of Table Mountain.

We were in a private room in the restaurant having dinner when my cell phone rang. I stepped outside on the balcony to take the call. It was a beautiful night in Cape Town and the stars and the lights of the city were shining bright. The call was from the Chairman/CEO of Boeing. He was calling from St. Louis where he had been in a meeting.

It was really surreal. I was standing on a balcony, outside of a restaurant at the top of Table Mountain, in Capetown, South Africa, located in the southern hemisphere. I was talking on a cell phone to the Chairman/CEO of Boeing who was in St. Louis, Missouri, in the northern hemisphere. He said, "Mr. Ambassador, I want to talk to you about our bid for the building of new planes for South African Airways."

I said, "Thank you very much. I'm pleased for your call and here are some thoughts I want to share with you about how we can win this bid." (I had memorized my notes about various approaches on how we could move this forward.)

He listened intently. As a matter of fact, it was so quiet on the other end, I said, "Are you still there?"

He said, "Yes, sir, yes, sir, Mr. Ambassador, I'm listening!"

I told him how we thought he needed to make changes on the ground and become more aggressive in marketing so they could win this bid.

Soon after that conversation, Boeing began to make changes on the ground by becoming more aggressive in their marketing efforts.

Boeing won the $2.3 billion dollar contract to build planes for South African Airways. This was fulfilling our mission of American investment in South Africa.

MY FIRST DÉMARCHE TO PRESIDENT MBEKI

Démarche is taken from a French word Démarcher meaning to march or to take a step.

In Diplomatic terms, it means a course of action or a political initiative.

I was asked by the State Department to deliver a démarche to President Thabo Mbeki relating to the country of Zimbabwe. There was a growing crisis around Mugabe's leadership in 2000, as elections were approaching in that country.

Zimbabwe is a land-locked country located in southern Africa between the Zambezi and Limpopo rivers. It borders South Africa, Botswana, Zambia and Mozambique. The President, Robert Mugabe, has led the country since 1980, following the end of minority white rule. At that time, the country that had been named Rhodesia after Sir Cecil Rhodes became known as Zimbabwe.

Mugabe was a revered leader who led the country to independence and sovereignty and to a more democratic government. The crisis in 2000 centered around land distribution in Zimbabwe.

President Mugabe encouraged the takeover of White commercial farms asserting that the land actually belonged to Black Zimbabweans. Turmoil followed with many killings of both White and Black Zimbabweans. It also prompted many Zimbabweans to flee their homes and to migrate into surrounding countries. This led to economic collapse and runaway inflation in the country.

Also in 2000, national elections were being held. With this backdrop, the U.S. government, through the State Department, had directed me to deliver a dèmarche to South African President Thabo Mbeki relating to the crisis situation in Zimbabwe.

It was the position of the U.S. government that we would like to see free and fair elections in Zimbabwe. Also, the U.S. had concerns about the crisis surrounding land redistribution and it was our hope for Democratic free elections.

Situations like this had been discussed in role-playing exercises during our two-week training program at the State Department in Washington. It was explained to us that it was permissible to read the démarche or to explain it's message in your own words.

I made an appointment with President Mbeki, through his Chief of Staff, Frank Chakane. I stated it was very important to meet with President Mbeki to deliver a very important message (démarche) concerning the crisis and upcomng elections in Zimbabwe.

Shortly thereafter, I received a call back from Frank Chakane that President Mbeki would like to hold the meeting at a military airbase near Pretoria as he would be landing there later in the evening. I was invited to bring any embassy officers of my choice to the meeting.

I discussed theses issues with the Political officer, Rita Ragsdale, and we confirmed the appointment for later that evening. President Mbeki arrived as scheduled, accompanied by the Minister of Trade and Industry, Alec Erwin. Rita Ragsdale and I greeted the President and the Minister. Then we were all escorted into a private room for the meeting. As we sat down and began the meeting, President Mbeki asked me if would like a "Scotch." I said, "No thanks, Mr. President, I'll just have water."

The meeting went on for over an hour and before the meeting was ended, I did have a "Scotch." I gave the démarche about Zimbabwe in my own words. It was well received by President Mbeki.

The political officer took copious notes making a record of our meeting. President Mbeki took this opportunity to explain what he wanted the U.S. government to know. This is the fascinating part of diplomacy. Even though I was there to give him the position of the U.S. government on Zimbabwe, he knew that I would report back. President Mbeki wanted to share his perception of what was going on in Zimbabwe. He wanted to educate America.

We listened for over 45 minutes as he gave a history lesson to educate us about the background of what was going on in Zimbabwe. The genesis of his lecture was the Lancaster House Agreement of December 21, 1979. This agreement allowed for the creation of the nation Zimbabwe. It also provided that a constitution be created. The distribution of land was one of the pivotal issues in this agreement.

From President Mbeki's perspective, the Lancaster House Agreement was never fully consummated. The agreement called for a system to compensate White farmers for their land and a fair process for redistribution. Neither of those things happened. He continued that while we may disagree with President Mugabe's tactics, there might be some underlying merit to his actions.

We went back to the embassy where the political officer put the notes together to send to Washington. In the notes, we discussed my delivery of the démarche as I was directed. We also made note of President Mbeki's position and his ideas about the why of Mr. Mugabe's move.

It was definitely an exciting diplomatic experience for me as I delivered my first démarche. It was also an educational experience as I learned the history of land issues in Zimbabwe from the President of South Africa.

BUSH VS. GORE
ELECTION IMPACT

> **"The American people have now spoken, but it's going to take a little while to determine what they've said."**
>
> *- President Bill Clinton*

As part of the Public Affairs and public outreach programs at the U.S. Embassy in South Africa, our Public Affairs team recommended topics of interest to share with the South African community. It was recommended that we focus and highlight the events surrounding the national election for President of the United States. In 2000, the race was between George W. Bush, the Republican Party nominee, and Al Gore, the Democratic Party nominee.

We set forth a public affairs information blitz where we invited South Africans and others to our sessions on the U.S. election process. We held panels and information sessions on the political processes unfolding in the campaign. It was our intent to educate South Africans on how our political system works. We rented hotel meeting rooms and a hotel ballroom in Johannesburg to set up information booths to publicize the events surrounding the elections.

We invited the South African press, print and media to stay with us and stay tuned as we official Americans sat through the late night and early morning waiting for the votes to be tallied.

We had real time newscasts coming in as the votes were being counted. We didn't realize at the time that the South African press would be so interested in our reactions as the votes were being counted and reported. Their camera eyes and listening ears were on our every word and expression.

We had talking heads from the networks in South Africa and in the United States. As the counting of votes progressed, things unraveled. There were complications in several states as to the counting of the votes; Florida was being highlighted particularly.

The challenges went on throughout the night and we were carrying this live as best we could so the South Africans could see our democratic system working. It appeared that the official result wouldn't be determined for hours, or maybe even days, so we decided to close down this outreach event and return to the embassy in Pretoria.

This election was very impactful on my situation as a political appointee as Ambassador to South Africa. The policy for political appointees is that we must submit our resignations if there's a change of administration.

After many weeks of confusion, the presidential election was decided with a legal decision made by the U.S. Supreme Court in favor of George W. Bush becoming President. I knew then that I would have to offer my resignation.

Gayle and I spent many hours discussing what my next steps might be as I wanted to remain for a while longer in South Africa to continue some programs I had started.

This would require that I be offered the opportunity by the new administration. Colin Powell was named by George W. Bush to be Secretary of State. I had known Colin Powell for years in Washington and respected him as a military general and as a person. Even though it was too early to tell what George W. Bush's policy might be toward Africa, I felt it would be worth while requesting more time in this position from the new administration.

I thought possibly I could continue working philosophically with this new administration if they allowed me to stay. Also, I had served on the board of Halliburton when Dick Chaney was President and CEO. Now George W. Bush had won with Dick Chaney as his vice president.

After discussions with Gayle, I asked for a conference with Colin Powell and later with Vice President Elect Dick Chaney to see if I could extend my stay as Ambassador to South Africa. After going back and forth with Colin Powell, he said that he did not see a problem but he would get back to me.

I managed to get back to the States in January 2001 and I scheduled a meeting in Washington with Vice President Elect Dick Cheney. It was a very cordial meeting and we talked about the possibility of extending my service in South Africa. He told me he did not see that as being a problem but he would have to talk to the "big guy" and that he would get back to me.

After some discussion, I'm sure between Vice President Elect Chaney and President Elect George W. Bush, I received word I could stay on as Ambassador to South Africa until my successor was confirmed.

Well, given my experience of eleven months in the confirmation process, I felt fairly secure that I would probably have at least another year as U.S. Ambassador to South Africa.

However, after several months, Gayle and I discussed whether I could support the foreign policy of this Bush Administration. After long talks, we agreed that it would be best for us to come out before my successor was confirmed.

So I made a call back to the African Bureau at the State Department and talked with the director, Ambassador Arlene Render, and told her I wanted to come out and resign my post. She said, "Oh no, why don't you think it over, wait 24 hours before you call me back."

I told her that I didn't need to think it over and that my mind was made up, but I did wait. The next day, I called Ambassador Render and told her that I had decided that I wanted to resign my post.

We scheduled my departure for June of 2001, giving me time to tie up loose ends and make the proper farewell calls. Fortunately for us, we were there and I was in my post when Secretary of State Colin Powell made a very important visit to South Africa in May 2001.

FAREWELL CALL ON PRESIDENT NELSON MANDELA

> "Nothing makes the earth seem so spacious as to have friends at a distance; they make the latitudes and longitudes."
>
> *- Henry David Thoreau*

Shortly before leaving my Ambassadorial post and South Africa, I made a farewell call on President Mbeki. I also made a farewell call on President Nelson Mandela.

I want to share that special moment with you because each time I share any moments spent in his presence, I feel so full of hope for the world, a feeling I just need to share.

I spent a year and a half in South Africa as the United States Ambassador. I met with Mr. Mandela on several occasions at his Johannesburg home office. He was a giant of a man and I was in awe whenever in his presence.

During that year and a half, I got to know his special assistant, Zelda LaGrange. We developed a good relationship friendly and official. I made a call to Zelda to arrange an appointment for my farewell. During that conversation, I asked her what she thought about a favor I wanted to ask of President Mandela and she asked what it was.

I told her I have four adult sons with families and I wondered if it would be appropriate to bring five copies of Mr. Mandela's book, *Long Walk to Freedom*, so he could sign one for Gayle and me, and then sign one for each son and his family. She said, "Sure! That would be fine."

We purchased the books and made a list of the names of our sons and their families. We were ready for our farewell appointment.

Gayle joined me at this appointment and we were both honored to be in his presence. I couldn't believe that as he autographed each book for the sons and their families, he wanted to know more about each son. As he came to each son's name, he'd say, "Tell me about him. What is he doing?" He listened with interest. I was so thrilled and pleased and honored that he shared this time with us.

DETOUR HOME

> **"The world is a book, and those who do not travel read only one page."**
>
> *- St. Augustine*

It was a bittersweet time after we decided that I should resign my post as U.S. Ambassador to South Africa. We traveled through Asia on our way home since neither of us had been to that part of the world. We were eager to get home to see our children and grandchildren, but we also wanted to spend time in Asia. So we studied long and hard about what countries we should visit and how long this trip should be.

I think in total our trip was close to three weeks. We went to Singapore and then to Hong Kong. We had not been to either country.

The Ambassador from Singapore to South Africa, Bernard Baker and his wife, Susan, had become our very good friends. When we told them about our plans to visit Singapore, they took over our itinerary. They wanted us to meet their families there and to spend time with them. They assured us that between the two families, they would take us around Singapore and make us very welcome. This all happened. We enjoyed being together as we ate wonderful Singapore food from the street vendors, visited the sites of Singapore and engaged in endless conversation.

In Hong Kong, we visited our dear friends the Danish Consul General, Peder Jensen, and his wife, Jette. We had known them for many years. We had a great visit staying with them in their lovely high-rise apartment in downtown Hong Kong. We relaxed by taking short trips, a fun and exciting boat trip to eat at the "Lamma Hilton" seafood restaurant on Lamma Island, did lots of walking in the city, and of course we ate and enjoyed such delicious food. It was a wonderful trip.

We arrived home in the U.S. on the West coast and got to see our families in California. After a short visit in California, we made our way to our residence in New Mexico before traveling east to visit our families in Maryland and Florida.

CONCLUSION

As my mind pauses and I take a deep breath, I begin to slow everything down and realize just how incredibly blessed I have been.

Together, with my very loving, independent, smart and compassionate wife, Gayle Jones Lewis, we have raised 4 four adult sons and now have 11 grandchildren and 1 granddaughter-in-law. All of them have their own personalities, ideas, passions and talents.

The view from my eyes as a husband, father and grandfather is an incredible one. From this perspective I can watch, assist when asked, and participate on many fronts.

No one's life is perfect. I am no different. There were many times I didn't believe in myself. It has taken me many years to escape the ego filled armor I wore as a shield.

I believe that everyone in their journey needs a sounding board of love, trust and truth. For me, it has been Gayle. Through thick and thin, good and bad, wrong and sometimes right, Gayle has always had my best interests in mind. She never wavered from telling me the truth and what I needed to hear. She consistently told me that my gift was simply being myself and that being ones self takes no effort. She has reinforced in me, the values of love, compassion and family.

I wrote this collection of memories for the sole purpose of sharing and reflecting on the life I have lived and continue to live. I find the more I reflect, the more I realize how fortunate I truly am.

I hope my memories will inspire many to take chances and live life with no regrets, move beyond your shortcomings and never let your past define you. I want to impress on you that it's okay to be scared and confused, misunderstood, and sometimes, not even liked. But none of that matters as long as you hold true to who you are and why you are.

Stay in your lane and focus on the gifts that make you happy and fulfilled. Life is too short for ongoing arguments and spending the bulk of your today focusing and worrying about what has long since passed.

And so, as I gaze out onto the beautiful mountains of New Mexico and reflect, the words

of an African proverb that I have held onto for
more than 50 years, remind me that -

No Condition is Permanent!

99135442R00117

Made in the USA
Columbia, SC
09 July 2018